Andrew

RUSSIA 1894–1941

HODDER EDUCATION
AN HACHETTE UK COMPANY

The Publishers would like to thank the following for permission to reproduce copyright material.

Photo credits: p. 10 © Viktor Karasev/123RF.com; **p. 14** © Everett Collection Historical/Alamy Stock Photo; **p. 31** © Granger Historical Picture Archive/Alamy Stock Photo; **p. 49** © Karl Bulla/ullstein bild via Getty Images; **p. 61** © Paul Fearn/Alamy Stock Photo; **p. 83** © Hulton-Deutsch Collection/CORBIS/Corbis via Getty Images; **p. 89** © Heritage Image Partnership Ltd/Alamy Stock Photo; **p. 106l** © Heritage Image Partnership Ltd/Alamy Stock Photo; **p. 106r** © ITAR-TASS News Agency/Alamy Stock Photo.

Acknowledgements

Every effort has been made to trace all copyright holders, but if any have been inadvertently overlooked, the Publishers will be pleased to make the necessary arrangements at the first opportunity.

Although every effort has been made to ensure that website addresses are correct at time of going to press, Hodder Education cannot be held responsible for the content of any website mentioned in this book. It is sometimes possible to find a relocated web page by typing in the address of the home page for a website in the URL window of your browser.

Hachette UK's policy is to use papers that are natural, renewable and recyclable products and made from wood grown in sustainable forests. The logging and manufacturing processes are expected to conform to the environmental regulations of the country of origin.

Orders: please contact Bookpoint Ltd, 130 Park Drive, Milton Park, Abingdon, Oxon OX14 4SE. Telephone: (44) 01235 827827. Fax: (44) 01235 400401. Email education@bookpoint.co.uk Lines are open from 9 a.m. to 5 p.m., Monday to Saturday, with a 24-hour message answering service. You can also order through our website: www.hoddereducation.co.uk

ISBN: 978 15104 1655 0

© Andrew Holland 2018

First published in 2018 by
Hodder Education,
An Hachette UK Company
Carmelite House
50 Victoria Embankment
London EC4Y 0DZ

www.hoddereducation.co.uk

Impression number   10 9 8 7 6 5 4 3 2

Year   2022 2021 2020

All rights reserved. Apart from any use permitted under UK copyright law, no part of this publication may be reproduced or transmitted in any form or by any means, electronic or mechanical, including photocopying and recording, or held within any information storage and retrieval system, without permission in writing from the publisher or under licence from the Copyright Licensing Agency Limited. Further details of such licences (for reprographic reproduction) may be obtained from the Copyright Licensing Agency Limited, www.cla.co.uk

Cover photo © IanDagnall Computing/Alamy Stock Photo

Illustrations by Integra Software Services Pvt. Ltd.

Typeset by Integra Software Services Pvt. Ltd., Pondicherry, India

Printed in India

A catalogue record for this title is available from the British Library.

Contents

Introduction — 5

Gateway to Russia in 1894 — 10

Chapter 1   The rule of Tsar Nicholas II — 11
Were the character, attitude and abilities of Nicholas II suitable for his role as tsar? — 12
How significant were the problems faced by Nicholas II in 1894? — 15
How serious was the opposition to Nicholas II from 1894 to 1905? — 18
To what extent were national minorities and Jews a threat to the authority of Nicholas II? — 22
How great an influence were Pobedonostsev and Witte on Russian government? — 25
What was the importance of the Russo-Japanese War for Russia? — 27
Why was there a revolution in 1905? — 30
What were the consequences of the 1905 Revolution? — 34
How successful were Stolypin's policies? — 37
How far had the political, economic and social situation in Russia improved by 1914? — 38
Study skills: Understanding the wording of the question and planning an answer — 42

Chapter 2   The 1917 Revolutions — 44
What was the impact of the First World War on Russia? — 46
Why was there growing opposition to tsardom? — 50
Why was there a revolution in March 1917? — 53
Why did the Provisional Government struggle to impose its authority? — 55
Why was there a revolution in October 1917? — 62
Study skills: Writing an introduction and avoiding irrelevance — 68

Chapter 3   The Civil War and Lenin — 72
How significant was the formation of the Constituent Assembly? — 73
How did Lenin begin to consolidate Bolshevik power? — 75
What were the causes and course of the Russian Civil War (1918–21)? — 79
Why did the Bolsheviks win the Civil War (1918–21)? — 85
How significant was the New Economic Policy (NEP)? — 89
How successful was the creation of the new communist government and the constitutions? — 91
To what extent was Lenin a strong leader of the Bolsheviks? — 93
Study skills: Avoiding descriptive answers, writing analytically and the importance of the opening sentence of each paragraph — 97

Chapter 4   The rule of Stalin — 99
Why is it important to consider Stalin's character and abilities when assessing his rise to power and policies? — 100
How important was the role of rivalries and divisions within the Bolshevik party in Stalin's rise to power? — 103
How effective was Stalin's use of propaganda and censorship in consolidating power? — 106
How effective was Stalin in creating a police state? — 109

      How successful were Stalin's agricultural policies in the 1930s?   113
      How successful were Stalin's industrial policies in the late 1920s and 1930s?   118
      Study skills: Writing a conclusion and overall essay writing   123

Revise, Review Reflect: Russia 1894–1941   125

Answering AS interpretation questions   127

Glossary   130

Index   132

Introduction

This book has been written to support your study of:
- The non-British Period Study Units Y219 and Y249, Russia 1894–1941
  This introduction gives you an overview of:
- the OCR AS and A Level course
- how you will be assessed on this unit
- the different features of this book and how these will aid your learning.

1 The OCR AS and A Level course

This study will form part of your History course for the OCR specification, of which there are three Unit Groups and a Topic-based Essay.

The Unit Groups comprise:
- British Period Study and Enquiry, which follow chronologically on from each other (Unit Group 1 – AS and A Level)
- a non-British Period Study (Unit Group 2 – AS and A Level)
- a Thematic Study and Historical Interpretations (Unit Group 3 – A Level only).

This book covers the non-British Period Study Topic Russia 1894–1941 from Unit Group 2 of the OCR History specification.

During this period, Russia underwent monumental changes with the removal of the Romanov dynasty, which had ruled the country for over 300 years and its replacement, initially by a provisional government, but then by the world's first Communist regime, with two revolutions occurring in 1917. The book explains the rule of the last tsar, Nicholas II, and his failure to deal with the challenges he faced, most notably the impact of the First World War. The short-lived Provisional Government was followed by the Bolshevik, or Communist regime, that was even more repressive than that of the tsars. The new Bolshevik government had to fight a bitter Civil War to gain control of the country, which resulted in the introduction of increased centralisation of power and the abandonment of any semblance of freedom.

The book explains how the result of the Bolshevik takeover led to the state's ever-increasing role. Under communist rule the country was modernised economically, notably under Stalin's leadership, but at a considerable cost in human life. A machinery of terror was developed so that opponents, or potential opponents were arrested, exiled or killed. However, this and the use of propaganda ensured that most people at least acquiesced in Stalin's rule and by the time the Soviet Union was attacked by Germany in 1941 it was able, eventually, to secure victory in the Great Patriotic War, which led ultimately to its emergence as a superpower. This book will analyse the degree of change and continuity from late tsarist Russia to the establishment and development of a Communist state.

The chapters in the book correspond to the Key Topics in the specification.

Introduction

2 How you will be assessed

A Level

Each of the three Unit Groups has an examination paper, whereas the Topic-based Essay is marked internally but externally moderated.
- Unit Group 1 – the British Period Study is assessed through two essays, from which you answer one, and the Enquiry is assessed through a source-based question. This counts for 25 per cent of your overall marks.
- Unit Group 2 – the non-British Period Study is assessed through a shorter answer essay and one essay. This counts for 15 per cent of your overall marks.
- Unit Group 3 – the Thematic Study and Historical Interpretations Unit is assessed through two essays, which cover at least 100 years, and one in depth question based on two interpretations of a key event, individual or issue that forms a major part of the theme. This counts for 40 per cent of your overall marks.

For the Topic-based Essay you will complete a 3000–4000 word essay on a topic of your choice. This counts for 20 per cent of your overall marks.

AS Level

Each of the two Unit Groups has an examination paper:
- Unit Group 1 – the British Period Study is assessed through two essays, from which you answer one, and the Enquiry is assessed through two source-based questions. This counts for 50 per cent of your overall marks.
- Unit Group 2 – the non-British Period Study is assessed through an essay and an interpretation question. The interpretation question will come from one of two specified Key Topics. This counts for 50 per cent of your overall marks.

Examination questions for Unit Group 2

For both the AS and A Level you will have been entered for a specific unit and your examination paper will contain only the questions relating to that unit.

In the A Level examination there is just one section. Two questions will be set and you must answer one. There will be two parts to the question; the short answer essay which carries 10 marks and the Period Study essay which carries 20 marks. You must answer both parts from the same question.

In the AS examination there will be two sections in the examination paper. Section A is the Period Study section and Section B is the Interpretation section. In Section A there will be two essay questions, both worth 30 marks and you will have to answer one of them. Each essay will be drawn from a different Key Topic, although the questions could be drawn from more than one Key Topic. In Section B there will be one Interpretation question, which will be drawn from one of the two Key Topics named in the AS Specification.

Questions on the Period Study

For AS and A Level questions on the Period Studies the types of questions set will be the same. Examples of questions using some of the more common command terms and specific requirements for each can be found at the end of each chapter in this book. The command terms are important and a key to success is understanding what these terms mean and what you have to do.

Command term	Description	Example in the book
Assess	Weigh up the relative importance of a range of factors and reach a **supported judgement** as to which is the most important	Page 18
To what extent	Consider the relative importance of the named issue by comparing it with other issues and **reach a balanced judgement** as to its relative importance	Page 39
How far	Consider the relative importance of the named issue and weigh up its role by comparing it with other issues to **reach a balanced judgement** as to its relative importance	Page 97
How successful	Consider a range of issues and make a judgement as to how successful each was before **reaching an overall judgement** about success	Page 36

Questions on the A Level short answer essay

The questions will be based on two key events, people or issues and you will be asked to explain which you consider to be of the greater importance, impact or significance for a particular issue. Questions will be structured in the following way:

Which of the following had more impact on the Russian economy during Stalin's rule to 1941?
  (i) **Collectivisation**
  (ii) **The first two Five Year Plans**

Explain your answer with reference to both (i) and (ii).

Questions on the AS Level Interpretation

The questions will be based around a short quotation from a historian. You will not need to know anything about the historian, but apply your knowledge of the issues raised by the quotation to evaluate the strengths and limitations of the quotation.

Questions will be worded as follows:

'Despite efforts at political reform, urban Russia on the brink of the First World War arguably found itself on the brink of a new revolution.'
O. Figes, *Revolutionary Russia 1891–1991*, 2014

Evaluate the strengths and limitations of this interpretation, making reference to other interpretations that you have studied.

Answering the questions

The AS examination is one and a half hours in length, but the A Level examination is one hour. In the AS, Section A carries more marks than Section B and therefore it would be sensible to spend about 50 minutes on Section A and 40 minutes on Section B. In the A Level, the Period Study essay, question (b) carries more marks than the short answer essay, question (a), and therefore it would be sensible to spend more time on the Period Study essay. Before you start any of the questions, make a brief plan. Advice on planning essays is given on pages 42–3.

The answers you write will be marked against the relevant mark scheme. It would be useful to familiarise yourself with these before the examination so that you are aware of the criteria against which your work will be marked. Mark schemes offer guidance, but they cannot cover

Introduction

everything and if you write something that is relevant and accurate, but not in the mark scheme, you will gain credit for it. You will be rewarded for well-argued and supported responses. Marks will not be deducted for information that is incorrect, but you should remember that incorrect knowledge may undermine your argument.

What will the examination paper look like?

The cover of the examination paper will tell you the level for which you have been entered, either AS or A Level. It will tell you the unit number, which for the AS is Y249 and for the A Level is Y219. It will also tell you the title of the unit, the date of the examination and the time allowed for the examination. The cover will also give you instructions about the answer booklet and the marks available.

3 About this book

At the start of the Period Study covered in this book there is a section called 'Gateway'. This provides a one-page summary of background material to the period you are about to study.

Each chapter in the book then covers one of the Key Topics listed in the OCR specification for the unit.

Chapters start with a brief introduction and a series of key questions. An overview of the period or theme of the chapter provides a brief introductory narrative along with a timeline which outlines the key events.

Key questions

The chapters are divided into sections, each addressing one of the key questions listed in the chapter introduction. The key questions may be broken down into sub-questions to help your understanding of the topic. By the end of the section you should be able to answer the key questions.

Key terms

The key terms that you need to understand in order to grasp the important concepts surrounding the topic are emboldened in the chapter the first time they are used and defined in the glossary on pages 130–1.

Activities

Throughout the book there are activities to help you develop the key skills needed for the examination such as developing analytical skills and making judgements.

AS Level

There are some elements of the AS examination in Unit 2 that are different from the A Level. The skills needed for AS Level questions are explained on pages 127–9.

Historical debates

As historians often disagree about the causes or significance of historical events or personalities, each chapter of the book has contrasting extracts from the writings of two historians. Not only will this introduce you to some of the key historical debates about the period you are studying, but also by using your historical knowledge and the information in the chapter you will be able to test the views of the historians in order to determine which view you find more convincing. There will also be a list of books for further reading on the issue. Knowledge of the debate is not necessary for the examination in Unit 2, but it will enrich your knowledge and help to develop a valuable skill, which is further tested in Unit 3 of the A Level.

Summary of the chapter

At the end of each chapter there is a bullet-point list of the key points covered in 'Chapter takeaways', which will help with revision.

Study skills

Each chapter has a Study skills section. These gradually help you to build up the skills you need for the examination papers, providing examples of parts of strong and weak responses and further questions and activities in which you can practise the skills.

Revise, reflect, review

At the end of the book there is a section that helps you to consolidate your understanding of the whole topic. It encourages you to think about the period as a whole and question many of your earlier views. There will also be further activities to help you prepare for the examination.

Gateway to Russia in 1894

You may not have studied any Russian history before; the Gateway below introduces you to some of the key issues that you will encounter in the early part of this book. The aim of the Gateway is to provide you with a basic understanding of these issues so that when you first come across them you will have some background knowledge from which to develop your understanding.

Society
- The landed gentry and nobility dominated society with only a small middle class.
- Serious social unrest over living and working conditions had been mounting (especially in the countryside) from the mid-nineteenth century.
- Tsars before Nicholas II implemented reforms to improve the working and living conditions of peasants.
- Despite being given freedom and access to land under Alexander II (1855–81) peasants were unhappy about the quality and quantity of land they were given.
- Peasants were controlled by village councils (the *mir*) headed by village elders.
- Urbanisation had started and an industrial workforce had begun to grow.

Economy
- Russia's economic growth had been sluggish in the nineteenth century and well behind that of the industrialised nations of Britain, Germany and the USA.
- Some industrial progress had been made but most industrial activity was small scale.
- Financial and banking sectors did not really exist in the modern sense.
- Much economic activity was related to agriculture.

Politics and government
- Russia was governed by a tsar, who was an autocrat and whose powers were said to be ordained by God.
- Members of the government were selected by the tsar.
- The government was based in St Petersburg.
- The elites in Russian society were concerned that Russia was falling behind Western Europe and would soon become a second-rate power.
- Governments made considerable use of the secret police to maintain order.

Empire
- The Russian Empire was spread over 8 million square miles (nearly 21 million km²); from west to east it was around 5000 miles (8000 km) and from north to south, about 2000 miles (3200 km), covering large parts of both Europe and Asia.
- The population had increased rapidly from 40 million in 1815 to 125 million by the time of the first official census in 1897.
- Most lived in European Russia with many moving to the main cities of St Petersburg and Moscow.
- Throughout the Empire there were many different races with their own languages, religions and cultures.
- National minority groups posed a threat to the tsars as most wanted independence.

Religion
- Religion was dominated by the Russian Orthodox (Christian) Church.
- The Church was a very conservative body that supported the authority of the tsar.
- As urbanisation got underway, the Church appeared more detached from the wants and needs of an expanding urban population.

Foreign relations
- For much of the nineteenth century Russia was feared by the West; its expansionist intentions were seen as threatening.
- Russia was concerned to exert its authority in the Caucasus region.
- Russia fell out with Austria but made alliances with France and Prussia.
- Russia was involved in two major wars between 1855 to 1894: the Crimean War (1853–56) and the Russo-Turkish War (1877–78).

The rule of Tsar Nicholas II

This chapter addresses the ability of Nicholas II, as tsar, to deal with the internal and external challenges he faced on coming to the throne. It considers how well equipped he was to deal with a faltering economy and rising social unrest and to balance those with his desire to maintain autocracy. The chapter assesses the success of the policies implemented by Nicholas. The chapter ends by looking at the situation in Russia by 1914 and considers whether it was in a stronger, more stable position than in 1894.

The chapter addresses a number of key questions.

- Were the character, attitude and abilities of Nicholas II suitable for his role as tsar?
- How significant were the problems faced by Nicholas II in 1894?
- How serious was the opposition to Nicholas II from 1894 to 1905?
- To what extent were national minorities and Jews a threat to the authority of Nicholas II?
- How great an influence were Pobedonostsev and Witte on Russian government?
- What was the importance of the Russo-Japanese War for Russia?
- Why was there a revolution in 1905?
- What were the consequences of the 1905 Revolution?
- How successful were Stolypin's policies?
- How far had the political, economic and social situation in Russia improved by 1914?

This chapter will also explain how to understand the wording of a question and how to plan a response to the question. It will focus on identifying the key words within the question and then explain how to ensure that you address the key demands of the actual question, rather than simply writing all you know about a topic.

Timeline

1892	August–May 1906	Sergei Witte's economic reforms
1894	November	Accession of Nicholas II
1897	October	Formation of the Jewish Bund
1898	March	Formation of Social Democrats (SD)
1900–02		Formation of Socialist Revolutionaries (SR)
1903	November	SD split into Bolsheviks and Mensheviks
1904	February–September 1905	Russo-Japanese War
1905	January	Bloody Sunday
	January–October	Revolution
	October	October Manifesto
1906	April	Fundamental Laws issued
1906	November–September 1911	Stolypin's reforms
1906	April–July	First *Duma*
1907	February–June	Second *Duma*
1907	November–June 1912	Third *Duma*
1912	November–February 1917	Fourth *Duma*
1911	September–July 1914	Period of social unrest
1912	April	Lena Goldfields incident
1914	July	Start of the First World War

Russia 1894–1941

Overview

When Nicholas II came to the throne in 1894, unlike his father and grandfather, he did not appear to have the personal qualities required to be a successful ruler. Although well-educated and intelligent, he lacked the dynamism and imagination to take Russia forward into the modern world. He adopted a number of conservative policies and did not appear to understand the magnitude of the problems that Russia faced.

Opposition to Nicholas II's rule proliferated, partly arising from his perceived weaknesses. Several political groups arose to organise the opposition: the radicals (Social Democratic Workers' Party [SD] and the Socialist Revolutionary Party [SR]); and the liberals (Kadets and Octobrists). The SD was to divide into the Bolsheviks and Mensheviks; it was the former, under their leader Lenin, which was to determine the fate of the Romanov dynasty.

Another challenge to Nicholas II's authority came from the national minorities in the Empire (in particular, the Baltic Germans, Poles, Finns, Armenians and Ukrainians). They had suffered as a result of the process of Russification (see page 22) and many were determined to break away from Russian control.

Nicholas II relied, early on, on two individuals to help him tackle economic, social and political issues. One was Konstantin Pobedonostsev, his ex-tutor, who retained a position as the chief minister in the Russian government until 1905. The other was Sergei Witte who was kept in position as minister of finance until 1903. Pobedonostsev emphasised the need for repression to be maintained and Witte focused on improving the state of the economy through developing state capitalism. However, to distract the attention of the people from growing economic and social problems, Nicholas engaged Russia in a disastrous war with Japan (1904–05). The consequences of this added to the discontent, coinciding with a period of intense social unrest in 1905. The events of 1905 culminated in the issuing of the October Manifesto, a statement of major political reform by Nicholas II and the establishment of a representative political chamber called the *Duma*. Although this appeared to be a step on the road to a constitutional monarchy, Nicholas came to distrust the *Duma* and severely restricted its composition and powers. In 1906, he published a set of Fundamental Laws, which confirmed that only he could sanction major legislative changes.

Nicholas went further in consolidating autocracy by appointing, in 1906, Peter Stolypin as chairman of the Council of Ministers. To deal with on-going land issues, Stolypin, from 1906 to 1907, introduced his policy of the 'wager on the strong' in an attempt at 'de-revolutionising' the peasantry. This was supplemented by repressive measures applied to those who felt that reforms were not as quick and as substantial as they had hoped.

By 1914, despite some economic progress, there was still a good deal of social unrest, as evidenced by the Lena Goldfields massacre of 1912. However, Nicholas appeared to be in quite a strong position given the way in which threats from political parties and the successive *Dumas* had been quelled and the growth of both the agricultural and industrial sectors.

Were the character, attitude and abilities of Nicholas II suitable for his role as tsar?

Nicholas II's character, attitude towards ruling and abilities are frequently seen as ill-suited to governing an empire that was striving to compete with the major world powers (the USA, Britain, France and Germany) of the time. His rule is usually considered a failure as it ended with his abdication, and led to the formation of a Provisional Government and a Bolshevik revolution that destroyed the old order. This view is rather unfair as it fails to take account of some of the entrenched problems Nicholas faced that had built up and that, by 1894, any tsar would have struggled to deal with.

Character

Nicholas II is often viewed by historians and his contemporaries as naive, stupid, lacking confidence, a bad judge of people and devious. The Soviet view of him was that he was cruel in the tradition of all Russian autocrats (hence the nickname 'Bloody Nicholas'). This view changed slightly in the post-Stalinist era when he was seen as having been a hapless bystander as the Romanov dynasty disintegrated in the face of pressure from the Russian peasantry and **proletariat**. Such views of the tsar's personality though are problematic for a number of reasons.

- Most judgements about the character of Nicholas seem to be based on his diaries. They provide details of everyday duties and events, and his meticulous approach to record keeping. Some historians have interpreted this as evidence of an obsession with orderliness, triviality and routine matters. However, the diaries give little indication of the mental state of the tsar.
- Nicholas was an intensely private and reserved individual. He gave away little about his true feelings and beliefs about being tsar.
- Other records suggest Nicholas was a pleasant, gentle person who disliked confrontation; this has been interpreted as meaning that the tsar was weak-willed and unable to make decisions.

Nevertheless, the behaviour of Nicholas II at certain times would suggest that some of the character traits listed above were apparent.

- He dealt with everyday affairs himself and had no private secretary. He insisted on starting his day by dealing with trivial matters, such as filing and putting the royal seal on envelopes for personal letters.
- This was often followed by a period of decision making, lasting for 90 minutes, over mundane issues, such as whether a wife should be allowed to live apart from her husband.
- Discussions with ministers over state affairs were last on the tsar's daily duty list. Even in a time of crisis, such as Russia's involvement in war generally, the tsar seldom prioritised discussions about what to do over ceremonial duties, family mealtimes and reading papers.

His sense of duty was especially evident when he took command of the Russian military during the First World War (see page 48) although his decision to enter the war could be seen as opportunism; it stirred up patriotism among the educated classes who were likely to endorse the personal style of rule of the tsar. Despite his commitment to engage in the war and then to personally take charge, Nicholas generally appears to have shown an aversion for power, which went against being an autocrat.

Attitude

Nicholas' attitude towards governing was based on faith in God, a sense of duty and a rigid belief in autocracy. The tsar, like his forebears, believed that religion and tsarism were inextricably linked. This was clearly shown in the Fundamental Laws of 1906 when it was stated that: 'The All Russian Emperor possesses the supreme autocratic power. Not only fear and conscience, but God himself, commands obedience to his authority.' Furthermore, Nicholas stated that it was his duty to 'uphold the principle of autocracy as firmly and as unflinchingly as did my ever lamented father'. Thus, adherence to the **dogma** of autocracy also meant that he prioritised maintenance of the Romanov dynasty.

> **Post-Stalinist era**
>
> The period after the end of the rule, in 1953, of the Russian leader Joseph Stalin (1879–1953).
>
> **Fundamental Laws of 1906**
>
> The tsar issued new orders about the constitution (how Russia was to be governed) that introduced some of the promised reforms of the October Manifesto but clearly stated the authority of the monarch.

Abilities

The character of Nicholas and his attitude towards tsarism make it difficult to see that he had the ability to rule. His overall weaknesses as ruler are often cited as the main reason for the downfall of the Romanov dynasty and the spiralling of Russia into revolution and **civil war**. However, Nicholas did show an ability to instigate reforms and to enforce them with a firm hand. It is sometimes the latter that has led to him being viewed as obstinate.

▲ Tsar Nicholas II and his family at the christening of tzarevich Alexei, 1904

Activity

Policy decisions that Nicholas made were the result of his personality and beliefs. It is therefore important that you have a clear understanding of his personality and beliefs and how they impacted on his policies. Complete the following table to help you summarise them.

Personality/belief	Impact on policy making
Autocracy	Would not allow the power of the tsar to be reduced

How significant were the problems faced by Nicholas II in 1894?

Nicholas II faced many political, economic and social problems in 1894.

Political

The political priority for Nicholas II was to preserve autocracy. However, the autocratic system, including the unwieldy bureaucracy, was vulnerable. Under the pressures of rapid industrialisation and urbanisation, the political system appeared inadequate. In particular:

- the regime seemed too preoccupied with routine paperwork
- it appeared isolated from its subjects due, in part, to inadequate communication systems
- the regime lacked an overall vision of how to manage change.

The old role of the state clashed with the demands for a new role, based on the requirements of industrialisation and urbanisation (see Table 1).

Table 1 Old and new roles of the state

Old role	New required role
Little interventionism	Aspects of the old role were still considered important
Defence of the realm	
Maintain order	Far more interventionism: managing economy; directing industry; providing more social services
Taxation	
Some extension to providing public with basic services	Clearer focus on education, healthcare, water supply, justice

To address the demands of industrialisation, an effective and efficient form of local self-government was needed to work in conjunction with a 'modern' system of central government. This required the development of professional roles, such as doctors, lawyers, educators, engineers and administrators. Such professionals, forming the core of what might be called a new 'civil society', were likely to demand a certain amount of autonomy and to challenge autocracy. The main political problem Nicholas faced was that he was unwilling to reconcile his desire to be an autocrat with the pressure for the reform of the Russian state.

There were occasions when Nicholas II did attempt to address this problem but he failed. This is illustrated by the establishment of the Department of Agriculture (1894), which was briefed to deal with mounting rural problems of poverty and unrest. It proved to be an ineffective institution and struggled to address the issues of land availability and distribution. This led to unprecedented levels of peasant rioting, especially in 1905–07.

There was also a rise in opposition to tsarism. Opposition had escalated due to the reactionary and repressive measures of Alexander III, Nicholas II's father. The Russian people were concerned about:

- the centralised control of the police under the **minister of the interior**
- the replacement of elected **justices of the peace** with **land captains**. (Land captains [landed gentry] were intended to impose control over rural Russia and could overrule local councils and judges. They were part of the Tsar's plan to reduce local democracy and to limit the power of the *zemstva* [provincial governments] and town councils. However, there is some doubt about whether the idea worked because of the shortage of suitable gentry and the opposition of local areas to state control.)

Zemstva

The *zemstva* (or regional councils) were introduced in 1864 by Tsar Alexander II. They were seen as an improvement on existing forms of local government as they were elected rather than chosen bodies. However, voting regulations meant that they were dominated by prominent landowners.

Alexander II 1818–81

Before Alexander II came to the throne in 1855, serious social unrest over living and working conditions had been mounting. Among the higher echelons of Russian society, there was concern that Russia was falling behind Western Europe and would soon become a second-rate power. This was especially the case after Russia's poor showing in the Crimean War (1853–56). Alexander II implemented a series of reforms, most of which stemmed from the **emancipation of the serfs** in 1861. Changes were made to local government, the military, the legal system, education and the economy. These seemed to constitute the start of a more liberal age, but did not prevent Alexander II from using repression to keep opponents in line. However, as the people became more liberated they appeared to threaten the security of the ruling elite and were clamped down on again. Alexander was assassinated in 1881 by a terrorist group, the 'People's Will'.

Russia 1894–1941

> ### Alexander III 1845–94
>
> Alexander III came to the throne in 1881 following the assassination of his father, Alexander II. A powerfully built man with a military manner, his period of rule is seen as one of reaction and repression in response to the more relaxed liberal period of his father, Alexander II. Many of the reforms prior to 1881 were abandoned. The 1881 Statute of State Security sanctioned greater use of repression. Russification (see page 22) was introduced to control discontent among national minority groups. This was a marked departure from the freedoms granted by Alexander II. Alexander III's reign was relatively peaceful and some positive economic reforms were carried out under Finance Minister Sergei Witte. However, Alexander never lived to witness the full impact of Witte's efforts as he died prematurely from kidney disease in 1894.
>
> ### Famine of 1891–92
>
> In 1891, the Minister of Finance, Ivan Vyshnegradsky, raised import duties to 33 per cent on a variety of goods including foodstuffs and at the same time encouraged grain exports. The net effect was less food available at higher prices. The resultant famine was the worst seen in Russia in the nineteenth century. Over 350,000 people died. The famine led to much public criticism of the tsarist regime but especially from the *zemstva*. By the time Nicholas II came to the throne, this criticism had started a campaign for further liberal reforms and was partly responsible for the growth of more widespread liberal opposition.

- a reduction of peasant representation in the *zemstva*
- an increase in censorship.

These concerns created problems for Nicholas. The resentment caused by the reactionary policies of Alexander III, which took away authority from the *zemstva* established by Alexander II, and the resentment about the authority at local levels of the land captains indicated to Nicholas that a challenge to his authority was brewing. There was also further political unrest among nationalist groups in the Empire, who were demanding autonomy and independence, and fear of the spread of liberalism and revolutionary ideas in Russia. Alexander III had simply repressed these problems and Nicholas II faced the difficulty of choosing between increased repression, which might cause discontent to grow, or concessions, which might endanger his beliefs in autocracy.

By 1905, both liberal and socialist opposition groups were calling for reforms to the political system to allow greater representation of the people. This culminated in the 'revolution' of 1905, which was significant as it led to reforms that appeared to reduce the autocratic powers of the tsar (see page 30).

Economic

Despite attempts by Alexander II and Alexander III to modernise industry, serious economic challenges still existed in 1894.

- **Productivity** was low compared with international rivals. Up to 1894, industrialisation had resulted in an average annual economic growth rate of 8 per cent, but much of this was achieved through small-scale enterprise (rather than larger-scale production based on the principle of the **division of labour**).
- There was some lack of free enterprise; the tsar and his ministers directed production by controlling the armaments industry and the railways – the main consumers of industrial products. However free enterprise was only important in the sense that the Western economic modernisation was associated with laissez-faire, free-market thinking. Although Russia did not have to follow this model, **Westernisers** demanded that the free market approach had to be copied whereas **Slavophiles** opposed this.
- A reliance on foreign investment, through the issuing of government bonds, tax exemptions and monopoly concessions to foreign investors, meant that the Russian government was never in total control of the rate at which industrialisation could occur. Russia was 'in the pocket' of overseas powers as there was always the risk that their financial aid would cease, although foreign investment did give a considerable boost to the tsarist economy.
- Exports of grain had been encouraged before 1894 to stimulate agricultural innovation and to support a more entrepreneurial approach to production. But, peasant productivity remained relatively low. This, and the grain export policy, contributed to the terrible famine of 1891–92 and exacerbated rural unrest.
- Other problems included the concentration of larger-scale enterprises only in the 'old staples' (iron/steel, mining and textiles), the small home market for goods, the lack of a flourishing middle class to provide sustained economic growth and an over reliance on state support. Russian technology lagged behind that of the more developed economies.

Nicholas II largely continued the policies of his predecessors. This compounded some of the more serious economic issues especially those connected with land utility.

Social

In 1894, Russian society was predominantly rural; about 80 per cent of the population were peasants. Referred to as the 'dark masses' by government officials, peasants were considered to pose a threat to the ruling elite because of the sheer size of this social group and how widely spread they were across the Empire. By the time Nicholas II became tsar, the fear of rural social unrest had heightened as a result of a number of developments.

- Despite the formation of a Peasants' Land Bank, in 1883, and the abolition of the peasant poll tax, in 1886, peasants were still aggrieved about their poor living standards.
- The Peasants' Land Bank had been designed to provide entrepreneurial peasants with funds at relatively low interest rates to purchase more and better quality land. But the redistribution of land had resulted in a reduction in the size of plots and the *mir* continued to be a barrier to innovation (even though the latter is what Russian officials demanded). The *mir* encouraged communal cultivation and restricted enterprise and innovation in the villages. There were problems of a rapidly growing population, rural unemployment and underemployment and famine. There were constant calls for a **repartition** of land as the 1861 emancipation had often reserved better land for the landowners. The unfair and unequal distribution of fertile land in Russia was a fundamental problem.
- The poll tax had been greatly disliked by peasants but its abandonment was still not enough to make up for the shortfall in incomes compared with the rising expenditure needed for the upkeep of farm plots.
- The 1891 famine resulted in the deaths of over 350,000 people; its impact was long lasting. Most of the hardship was suffered by those in the countryside and it was remembered for decades to come.

> **Peasants' Land Bank (established 1883)**
> A bank specially set up by the government to allow peasants to borrow money at relatively cheap interest rates to allow for the purchase of land.
>
> **Poll tax (abolished 1886)**
> A tax per head of the population. The Russian poll tax had been in place since 1718.

The first official census taken in Russia, in 1897, revealed that social issues were not confined to rural life.

- The industrial workforce had started to grow; by 1890 it had already reached 1.4 million and doubled to 2.9 million by 1912. This signalled the rise of a new class of industrial workers. The problem for the tsar was that this new 'class' developed a political awareness (or consciousness), due to their geographical proximity to each other, poor working and living conditions. They soon found a voice through socialist organisations to challenge the authority of the tsar. By the early twentieth century, this challenge was most evident in the form of strikes and mass protest meetings.
- Industrialisation led to urbanisation and associated public health problems, such as poor housing, lack of sanitation and inadequate water supplies. The result was the spread of diseases, especially cholera. This added to the list of grievances, against the regime, that the proletariat started to formulate.
- Social change revealed a link between the changing wants and needs of new groups and the inability of Russian government to meet them. Although the Ministry of Finance went some way to protecting workers by resourcing the establishment of a factory inspectorate, the Ministry

of Internal Affairs started to take a more aggressive stance towards any attempts to support the labouring classes. Thus, there was confusion and inconsistency in the government's stance on labour relations.

In conclusion, the political, economic and social challenges faced by Nicholas overlapped to form a substantial threat to autocracy.

Activity

1 Consider the following question:
Assess the importance of the challenges faced by Nicholas II on his accession in 1894.

Complete the following table, which could serve as a plan for an answer to the question (an exemplar of how you might proceed is included).

Factor	Degree of importance (out of 10: 0 being lowest)	Explanation	Link to other factors
Political – Nicholas II's unswerving belief in autocracy	7	Nicholas was reluctant to share his authority but, as the Russian Empire grew, devolution and distribution of power became increasingly necessary	**Political** – those who wanted Russia to modernise started to question the tsar's authority **Economic** – autocracy was not always compatible with entrepreneurial activity (the freedom to innovate, for example)

2 Now write an introduction to the question that sets out your line of argument. Make sure you include a view about the greatest challenges faced by Nicholas II.

The Revolution of 1905

Tensions had been building up in Russia with various groups having grievances against the regime. After Russian defeats by Japan (1904–05) and troops firing on protestors in St Petersburg in January 1905, the tsar faced revolutionary agitation. Forced to agree to a new national assembly and to legalise political parties, the tsar nevertheless regained control because of the loyalty of his army and divisions among the opposition.

Peter Struve 1870–1944

Struve was from a distinguished academic family in Perm. Initially, a keen Marxist he rejected these views and founded a liberal magazine. Returning in 1905, he founded the Constitutional Democratic Party. He opposed the Bolshevik Revolution of 1917 and lived in exile in Paris.

How serious was the opposition to Nicholas II from 1894 to 1905?

Opposition to the tsar arose partly in the form of political groups, which had started to form illegally during the rule of Alexander III. It certainly posed a real threat as it pressurised Nicholas to make concessions that reduced his autocratic powers. The tsar's response was to attempt to take back authority through the use of Fundamental Laws (1906) and physical force.

Opposition groups had developed illegally during the reign of Alexander III. They came to pose a threat to the regime during the Revolution of 1905 (see on the left) when Nicholas II was forced to make concessions which made political parties legal. The main groups that developed were the Liberals, Populists and Marxists.

Liberals

By 1894, liberal Westernisers (as opposed to Slavophiles) continued to demand that Russia should be governed in a similar way to Western European democracies, such as Britain. Liberal ideas had been supported by the emergence of the *zemstva*, and the mid-1890s revival of the concept of a *zemstvo* union. In 1904, Peter Struve founded the Union of Liberation, which demanded greater freedoms and justice for all Russians. In particular, the Union wanted fairer land distribution for peasants, a representative constituent assembly and improved conditions for industrial workers. These were all issues that would, if addressed, have diluted the authority of Nicholas.

Kadets and Octobrists

An extension of the liberal movement occurred within a decade of Nicholas' coming to power. After the 'revolution' of 1905 (see pages 34-6), the clamour for a **constitutional monarchy** grew with the formation of the Constitutional Democrats (Kadets). Led by Paul Milyukov, this was the intellectual arm of the liberal movement, and would play a very important role as opposition within the first *Duma*. A more moderate liberal group also emerged, called the Octobrists. These were individuals, such as Alexander Guchkov and Mikhail Rodzianko, who displayed loyalty to the tsar, but who wanted changes to the system of government. The Octobrists, in particular, supported Nicholas II's October Manifesto (see page 33) and were therefore criticised by more revolutionary organisations. Overall, the liberal movement posed little threat; it involved a relatively small number of people, mainly middle class, had no organised political party and had only limited ways of expressing their concerns effectively. They had little support from the peasants and therefore only limited influence on policies.

Populists

The Populists (also referred to as *Narodniks*) were revolutionaries, who emerged in the 1870s. They argued that agricultural communes and co-operative workshops would provide a base for the Russian economy to develop without resorting to capitalism. By 1894, they appeared not to pose much of a threat as they had failed to mobilise large-scale support. They largely consisted of young intelligentsia, who thought they would be able to preach to peasants to convince them to change the way Russia was ruled. This had little success in rural communities and peasant insurrection did not materialise. However, from the Populist movement the Socialist Revolutionaries (SR) of the early twentieth century emerged; this was important as it marked a shift in attempts to represent the interests of people in the new urban areas of Russia.

The Socialist Revolutionaries

The SR developed from the Populist movement, focusing on improving the living conditions of the poorest in society, including the growing urban proletariat. The Socialist Revolutionary Party was formed in 1901, and led by the intellectual Victor Chernov. By 1905, the group had split into the a more radical left-wing and a moderate right-wing. The left employed direct action; from 1901 to 1905 they were responsible for about 2000 political killings, including Grand Duke Sergei and Vyacheslav Plehve. The right worked with other parties and groups, gathering support and momentum after the 1905 revolution. The right appealed to peasants, whereas the left focused on the plight of industrial workers. Despite the divisions, the SR had the most support of the opposition parties and were the biggest threat to tsarist rule before the October 1917 revolution.

Paul Milyukov 1859–1943

Milyukov, a historian, served as foreign minister in the provisional government in 1917. He was a member of the intelligentsia and founder of the Kadets (1905). Milyukov was a well-known critic of the tsar.

Alexander Guchkov 1862–1936

Guchkov served as minister for war and navy in the provisional government in 1917. He was a wealthy industrialist and founder of the Octobrists (1905). Although respectful of tsarism, he was a critic.

Mikhail Rodzianko 1859–1924

Rodzianko was a wealthy Ukrainian landowner. A monarchist who used his position as president of the *Duma* to try and make links between the tsar and his subjects. He warned the tsar of the dangers of an uprising in 1917 and was ignored. For a short time, he headed the Provisional Government. He opposed the Bolshevik take over and was forced to flee to Serbia.

Grand Duke Sergei 1864–1905

Fifth son of Alexander II and brother of Alexander III. From 1891, he was assassinated by the SR in 1905.

Vyacheslav Plehve 1846–1904

The much-hated minister of the interior who served from 1902 to 1904. Assassinated by the SR in 1904.

Marxists

Another revolutionary group, the Social Democrats (SD), emerged at the same time as the SR. They based their ideology on the writings of Karl Marx, believing that the proletariat could be 'educated' to overthrow Russian autocracy by revolution.

Viktor Chernov 1873–1952

Chernov was the son of a former serf from Samara. He studied law in Moscow and became a radical populist. He joined the Socialist Revolutionaries in 1901 and was deeply interested in land reform. An SR leader in the *Duma*, he became minister of agriculture in the Provisional Government of 1917 and chairman of the Constituent Assembly. He opposed Lenin and had to flee into exile. He died in the USA.

George Plekhanov 1856–1918

Plekhanov was from a noble family but became a populist and opponent of the tsar. He founded the first Marxist party in Russia and initially supported the Bolsheviks, but he rejected Lenin's ideas on party discipline in 1905 and opposed the October revolution.

Karl Marx 1818–83

Marx was born on 5 May 1818 in Trier in western Germany. His father was a successful Jewish lawyer (although he converted to Christianity to help him progress in his career). Marx followed his father, studying law in Bonn and Berlin, but also became interested in philosophy, especially the works of Hegel and Feuerbach. He then started a career as a journalist and moved to Paris, France, where he believed his writings on class struggle and revolution would gain a wider audience. There he met Friedrich Engels, the son of a wealthy factory owner, with whom he collaborated to develop ideas about revolutionary communism.

Marx's radicalism saw him expelled from France; in 1845 he moved to Brussels, Belgium, where he continued his partnership with Engels. Together they produced the famous *Communist Manifesto* (published in 1848). Its main message was that 'the history of all hitherto existing society was the history of class struggle'. The ultimate class struggle would be between capitalists and the proletariat (industrial workers); revolutions would occur that would lead to the rule of countries by workers ('dictatorship of the proletariat'). However, the proletariat would then have to fend off opposition before their ultimate aim could be achieved; the establishment of a classless society. The historical process of change would then come to a halt.

In 1849, Marx moved to London with his family and was again followed by Engels. Marx was plagued by illness and a lack of funds; he relied on Engels to help him develop his ideas. In 1867, the first volume of *Das Kapital* was published. This set out some of Marx's key ideas on political economy, especially those concerning the Labour Theory of Value. The remaining volumes were published after Marx's death, having been edited by Engels.

In his later years, Marx became less productive as a writer. In 1881, he became depressed by the deaths of his wife, Jenny, and one of his daughters. He died on 14 March 1883 and was buried at Highgate Cemetery, London.

The Social Democrats

In 1898, the All-Russian Social Democratic Workers' Party was founded in Minsk. The group was influenced by an interpretation of Marx's work made by George Plekhanov, who emphasised the need to encourage working-class consciousness. However, since few workers had the time or interest to engage with Marxist theory, some SD supporters focused on more practical concerns, especially improving pay and lowering working hours. Julius Martov and Vladimir Ulyanov (Lenin) were the main instigators of SD attempts to improve conditions for workers, although Lenin soon became frustrated by how ineffective their efforts appeared to be. Lenin therefore called for more revolutionary tactics to be deployed. In 1901, he produced a pamphlet called *What Is to Be Done?* It outlined the idea that a complete overthrow of the tsarist system of rule could be achieved by workers if they were led by a politically educated elite or vanguard. On paper this obviously posed a serious threat to

Nicholas II but in reality, at least in the short term, it had minimal impact. There were two reasons for this.

- Lenin's views caused a division in the SD movement between the **Mensheviks** and the **Bolsheviks**. The former wanted to continue to work for political, economic and social change within the 'system' whereas the latter argued that workers were capable of being sufficiently politically educated to create a revolution.
- Nicholas II attempted to quell worker fears about deteriorating working and living conditions by authorising, in 1902, the creation of legal workers interest groups (known as Zubatov Unions after their 'designer', S.V. Zubatov, chief of the Moscow secret police). The idea was that workers, through the unions, would be able to negotiate with state officials to improve their plight. Very soon though, the unions became unruly and unmanageable. By the summer of 1903, the Zubatov plan was abandoned. Nevertheless, it did give indication that worker unrest needed to be taken seriously.

Sergei Zubatov 1864–1917

Zubatov was a revolutionary who turned informer. He went on to join the secret police (*Okhrana*) and to become its head. In 1901, he initiated workers' organisations financed by the tsarist state to control agitation – the Zubatov Unions – but Minister of the Interior Plevhe disbanded them in 1903 and Zubatov was sacked. He killed himself in 1917 when the tsar abdicated.

V.I. Lenin 1870–1924

Lenin (Vladimir Ilyich Ulyanov) studied law at university where he started to develop his ideas about revolution. His radical pronouncements and associations with prominent revolutionaries resulted in his exile to Siberia in 1897. In 1900, he joined the Social Democratic Party and in 1903 led the Bolsheviks as a breakaway group. Lenin returned to Russia to witness the 1905 'revolution' but was not actively involved and a year later he was again exiled. He returned to witness the aftermath of the turmoil of February/March 1917 and was then removed from Russia only to return to lead the Bolshevik revolution in October. After this, he consolidated Bolshevik rule and ensured victory in the Civil War. From 1922, Lenin was immobilised after a number of strokes and died in 1924. Despite often being in exile, Lenin had a great influence on the revolutionary movement through his writings and actions and was instrumental in the Bolshevik seizure of power and the establishment of communist rule in Russia. Some historians believe that Lenin laid a firm foundation for future communist leaders to build on.

Despite the Bolshevik's fairly frequent use of terrorism to achieve their aims (such as the armed robbery of banks to gain funds), the authorities seemed not to take them too seriously. The police did not report on the Bolsheviks being a threat to state security. This notion of a limited threat is partly supported by membership figures: in the period before 1914, the number of those claiming to be Bolsheviks varied from 5000 to 10,000. Even in the tumultuous months of February to August 1917 the figure probably never rose above 25,000. However, caution should be taken in using such statistics: are the numbers over- or under-estimates?

However, it was rising worker radicalism that caused the tsar to allow, on the one hand, the legalisation of political parties (1905) and, on the other, the use of repression if protests appeared to be getting out of hand.

Overall, it is difficult to measure the extent of the threat posed by political opposition groups due to the lack of reliable quantitative evidence. Some judgements can be based on the behaviour of different opposition groups and how the regime reacted to this. This would lead to the kind of conclusion drawn by the historian Sarah Badcock who has pointed out that for Nicholas II, 'the notion that social unrest reflected a broader need for change went unheeded'.

Russia 1894–1941

Activity

This section has focused on the threat of the opposition groups to Nicholas II. Re-read the section on opposition and use the information to help you complete the table below, which will help you assess the threat.

Opposition group	Evidence they were a threat	Evidence they were not a threat	Mark out of six: 0 = no threat, 6 = serious threat	Judgement on threat

1 Which group do you think were the most serious threat to Nicholas II? Explain your answer.
2 In light of the information in your table, how serious do you think the threat to Nicholas was?
3 Draw up an essay plan for the question 'How serious a threat to Nicholas II was the opposition in the period from 1894 to 1905?'

To what extent were national minorities and Jews a threat to the authority of Nicholas II?

By the start of the nineteenth century, the Russian Empire consisted of Great Russia and 'national minorities', that is, those who did not originate from the Russian peoples (see Figure 1). The most prominent national minority groups were from: Poland, Finland, the Caucasus and Central Asia, and the Baltic Provinces (Estonia, Latvia and Lithuania). The first Russian census of 1897 revealed the significance of such groups; for example, it revealed that 55 per cent of the population of the Ukraine consisted of minorities. Russian Jews stood out as a unique minority as their geographical location was artificially created (The Pale: the band of territory in Poland, Ukraine and south-western Russia where Jewish settlement was permitted) and crossed the boundaries of other groups.

Not all national minorities opposed the ruling elite under Nicholas II. The Finns, Baltic Germans and Christian Armenians remained fairly loyal, whereas the Poles, Ukrainians and Tartars were a problem for Russian rulers. The main objective of the 'unco-operative' national minorities was to gain autonomy or even break away from Russian rule and gain independence. Subsequently, many of the minorities were subjected to a policy of Russification to lessen their threat to the tsar's authority.

Russification

The process that aimed to merge all of the nationalities of the Empire into one nationality of pure 'Rus' (who were the founders of the first Russian state, who ruled over the native Slavonic tribes). It was a key tsarist policy after 1881. The tsars believed it would lead to a stronger and more united empire.

The rule of Tsar Nicholas II

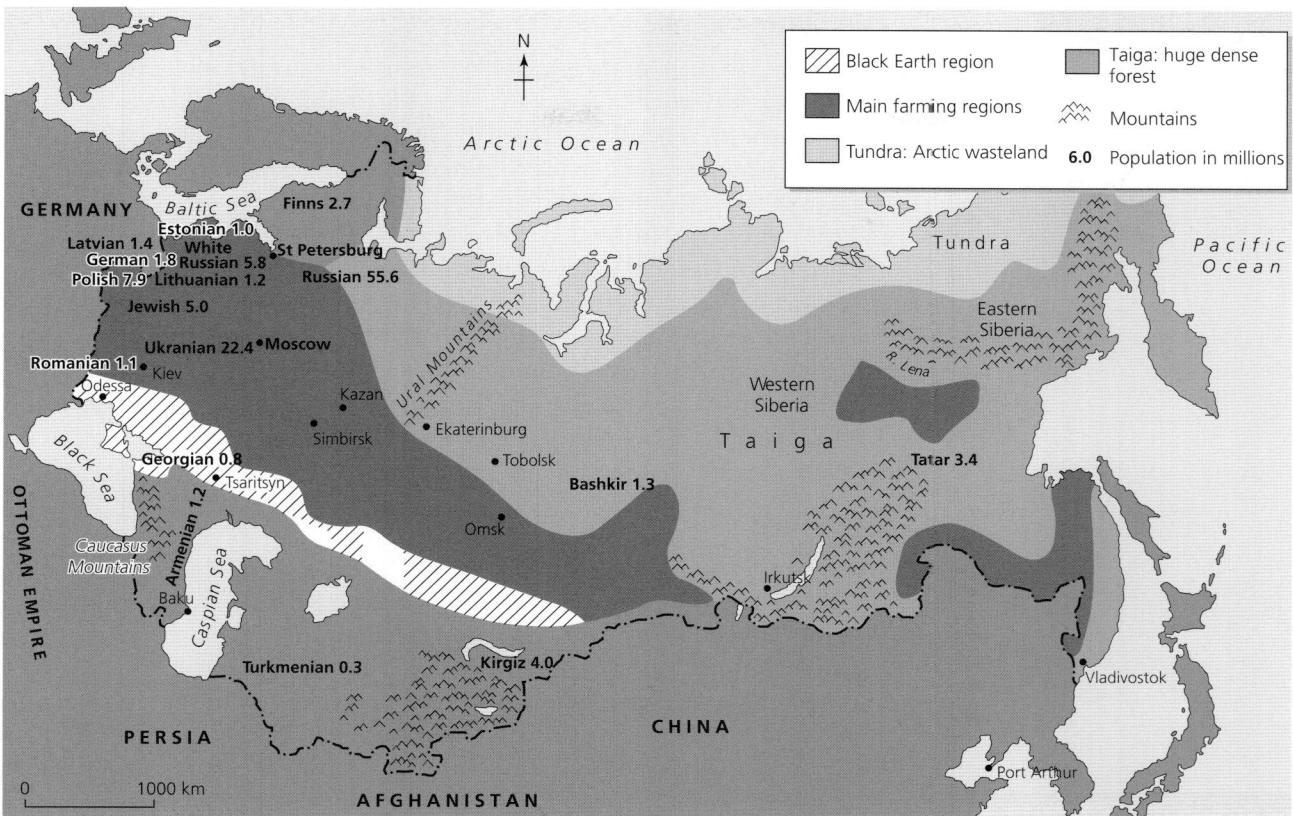

Figure 1 The Russian Empire in 1900 showing the population of national minorities

The Poles

Poland had a long history of wanting to break away from Russian influence. The Polish Revolt of 1863 was an indication of the seriousness of the threat of nationalism. It led to the first major attempt to russify a part of the Empire and led to the policy of control being implemented on a wider scale. However, as a result of industrialisation in Poland, by the 1890s, a distinct proletariat emerged that showed an interest in Marxism and socialism. Workers' political parties were formed (the Polish Socialist Party, 1892, and the Social Democratic Party, 1893), indicating that the Polish government was willing to listen to workers concerns. Nationalism also re-emerged, as indicated by the formation of the National Democrat Party. Polish politicians elected from these groups made important contributions to the first and second *Dumas* (see page 35). That Nicholas allowed this political activity suggests that he was willing to trust Polish politicians to toe the line and to ensure Poland remained an integral part of the Empire. This lessened the threat they presented towards his authority.

The Ukrainians

Nationalism was not as strong in the Ukraine as in Poland, but Ukrainians still looked to build a separate cultural identity, which was reflected in their literature and the arts. In response, Nicholas II continued the policy of Russification in the Ukraine.

The Caucasians

Those living in the Caucasus region of Russia were divided along religious lines. Some, such as the Armenians, were Christians, while others, such as the Chechens, were Muslims. These divisions, coupled with the high level of illiteracy in the region, made continued Russification under Nicholas II relatively easy. Nevertheless, Populist movements (such as the Dashnaks and the Georgian Mensheviks) emerged to oppose Nicholas II's repressive measures. The Dashnaks organised self-defence military units to combat intrusions by Russian officials. The Mensheviks in Georgia provoked the rise of a nationalist movement but, more significantly campaigned for Georgia to ally with Germany in the hope that if the latter were to win in a war with Russia, Georgians would automatically be freed from Russian control. Overall, the peoples of the Caucasian region posed a significant and continuous threat to the tsar's authority.

The Finns

The appointment by Nicholas II of Nikolai Bobrikov as governor general marked a change in fortune for the Finns. Before 1894, the tsars had adopted a liberal view on Finland. An allowance was made in 1861 for the creation of a separate Finnish parliament (Diet) followed, in 1865, by a constitution. Under Bobrikov though, Finland was fully integrated into the Russian Empire and Russified. This provoked much opposition and, as a result, in 1905, Finland was given full autonomy. However, this was quickly reneged on by Peter Stolypin in the same year. Finland eventually gained independence once more, like Poland and the Ukraine in 1917, but for the majority of Nicholas II's rule the tsar neglected demands for greater freedoms, clamping down on attempts to resist the Russification process.

Peoples from the Baltic Provinces

By 1894, the Baltic Provinces were still strongly influenced by 'old' German landowning nobility and gentry. The states were relatively stable and prosperous because of the abundant supplies of raw materials used in a range of industrial activities. Riga, in Latvia, became a very important commercial and business centre. As a result, many native Russians migrated there. This prompted Nicholas II to pay attention to the possibility of a growth in a separatist movement in the region. But as many native Russians migrated to the Baltic Provinces, in search of higher wages and more regular employment, Russian economic influence naturally increased in the area. This made Russification a logical and inevitable process. German influence waned by the end of the century which appeared to spark a rise in nationalism among native Estonians, Latvians and Lithuanians. Pressure from these areas was still not enough for full independence to be considered.

The Jews

The Jews in Russia were not so much a national minority as a religious one. Jews never appeared to pose much direct opposition to Nicholas II. It was a perceived threat that resulted in them being treated so badly. Nicholas II continued the anti-Jewish position taken by his father. They were accused of being 'revolutionaries' as some were affiliated to the SD and there was indeed a separate Jewish SD Party called the *Bund*. As a result running up to 1905 a **pogrom** in the Pale of Settlement occurred.

Peter Stolypin 1862–1911

In 1906, Stolypin was minister of the interior, but soon rose to prime minister (1906 to 1911). He proved to be an authoritarian administrator, although he was quick to respond to the changing political climate in Russia. He is best known for introducing the Peasants Land Bank and land reforms (including the attempted break-up of the *mir*, see page 37). Such positive developments were countered by the high degree of repression authorised by Stolypin. This was evident through anti-Jewish pogroms and the introduction of martial law in 1906. The latter resulted in about 2500 executions between 1906 and 1911; the hangman's noose at the time was jokingly called 'Stolypin's necktie'. He was assassinated in Kiev in 1911.

Of particular note was the following:
- The issuing by the secret police, in 1902, of the 'Protocols of the Elders of Zion'. This was a theory that Jews were plotting, across the world, to subvert the governance of nations (especially in Europe) and create their own police states.
- The wave of pogroms in 1903 that began in Kishinev, Bessarabia. In two days, 47 Jews were murdered, about 400 wounded and over 1300 properties (houses and shops) destroyed.

The treatment of Jews stemmed from ordinary Russians' innate fear of foreigners. Although Nicholas, by turning a blind eye to such behaviour, could be seen to have promoted it. However, despite Nicholas' dislike of Jews, he made a concession by allowing them to sit on the *Duma*.

Activity

1. Complete the following table to provide an analysis of the level of threat posed by minorities to the authority of the tsar

Minority group	Mark out of ten: 0 = no threat, 10 = serious threat	Explanation of judgement

2. Now complete the following table to show how effectively Nicholas II dealt with minorities. Think about how the term 'effectively' can best be defined and measured.

Minority group	Very effectively (explanation)	Not very effectively (explanation)

How great an influence were Pobedonostsev and Witte on Russian government?

Konstantin Pobedonostsev had some influence on Nicholas II through his role as chief procurator of the Holy Synod; he encouraged him to adhere to autocracy and orthodoxy. Sergei Witte had a greater influence on policy: in particular, as minister of finance he promoted a liberal approach to economic development. However, like Pobedonostsev, he held a conservative view on politics. Both sanctioned repression as a tool to keep dissidents in check.

Pobedonostsev's influence on Russian government

Pobedonostsev achieved much as an official and adviser to the tsars although most of his influence was before 1894. In particular, as tutor to Nicholas II, he was in a position to indoctrinate the young heir to the throne in the principles of orthodoxy, autocracy and nationalism. His influence on Russian government after 1894 was more indirect than direct.

However, he influenced Nicholas II's rule in the following ways.
- He helped prepare judicial reforms for the tsar in 1864, which stayed in place after 1894.
- He became an adviser and writer on Russian law. From 1868 to 1880, he published the three volumes of *A Course of Civil Law*. These texts influenced the training of Russian legal experts in the reign of Nicholas II.

Protocols of the Elders of Zion

The Protocols was a crude anti-Semitic forgery that purported to be a record of a meeting of Jewish leaders in the late nineteenth century to plan world domination. It appeared in Russia around 1902/03 and was used to justify attacks on Jews, though it was rejected by the tsar as untrue.

Konstantin Pobedonostsev 1827–1907

Pobedonostsev had gained a thorough grounding in the Russian governmental, administrative and legal system through his time at the St Petersburg School of Jurisprudence. In 1865, he became tutor to Alexander II's son and therefore influenced how the Tsar's heirs would rule. By 1868, he was working as a senator, which gave him greater access to the judicial process. A conservative and reactionary, he was an advocate of autocracy and enemy of liberal democracy. He balked at the changes Nicholas II proposed in the October Manifesto of 1905. Devoutly religious, he venerated the Russian Orthodox Church. He advocated that all peoples of the Empire should be Orthodox Christians, which helps explain his anti-Jewish sentiments. His ultra conservative approach to religious matters was expressed, from 1880 until his death, through his role as chief procurator of the Holy Synod. But, as with his views on legal and political reform, there was opposition to the religious stance that he took on Jews. However, his influence faded during the reign of Nicholas II.

Russia 1894–1941

> **Sergei Witte 1849–1915**
>
> After an unspectacular period at school, Witte went on to study science and mathematics at university in Odessa in the Ukraine (1866–70). From 1870 to 1892, his career focused, as a government official, on the development of Russia's railways and communications; from 1889 to 1891, he was director of railways. In 1891, he became minister for transport, followed by minister for finance in 1892. Witte remained in control of Russian financial matters, under Nicholas II, until 1903, when he was transferred to the Committee of Ministers to act as chairman. In 1905, he was appointed as president (the equivalent of prime minister) of the Council of Ministers and helped negotiate peace with Japan to end the Russo-Japanese War, but, in 1906, he was forced to resign from this position. Witte was not involved directly in economic and political affairs after this time.

- He was a major influence on Alexander III's policy making and manifesto. Nicholas II continued with many of these policies, such as those focused on national minorities and Jews.
- He became the chief procurator of the Holy Synod (1880); this allowed him to advise the tsar on religious matters, and to influence the Church and educational and social policies. As chief procurator, Pobedonostsev was able to encourage Nicholas II to be consistent in his proclamations about being placed on earth to rule autocratically as a result of the will of God.

However, after 1894, the clamour for reform from both within and outside government went against the chief procurator's preaching. Although he continued to have some influence on religious policy, Pobedonostsev became less of a political force. His influence waned as he was seen as an ultra-conservative and against modernisation. He had some support from Slavophiles but none from the growing number of liberal thinking Westernisers. His reactionary stance on the economy and society had the potential to cause further divisions in the political ranks and he was therefore largely ignored by Nicholas II. Compared with Witte, Pobedonostsev had no significant direct influence on Russian government after 1894.

Witte's influence on Russian government

Witte's influence on Russian government came mainly through his success as a finance minister. Witte's appointment as minister for finance in 1892 marked a distinct break from the past. Previous ministers had attempted to stimulate Russian industrialisation but their achievements had been limited. Witte's appointment changed this. By 1892, Russian economic activity still focused predominantly on agricultural production. Witte was the first to show total commitment to industrialisation in an attempt both to compete with other industrialised nations and to improve Russian military capability. This was to be achieved mainly at the expense of agriculture (part of the so-called 'substitution' effect; investment capital was substituted or directed from agriculture to industry), which caused suspicion and consternation among sections of the Russian elite. Witte claimed that 'all thinking Russia was against me', which emphasises how radical he considered his approach.

There were four main strands to Witte's approach to finance and the Russian economy.

- The resurrection of Reutern's idea of encouraging foreign experts to come to Russia.
- A return to taking out foreign loans (negotiated in 1906, when serving in the Council of Ministers), raising taxes and interest rates to boost available capital for investment in industry.
- The belief that placing Russian currency, the rouble, on the **Gold Standard** would achieve financial stability (this was done in 1897).
- An insistence that most state investment focused on heavy industry and the railways.

Witte's views and actions provided the base for the 'Great Spurt' in economic activity, which boosted the international prestige of the Russian government. The 'Great Spurt' appeared to show Russia had emerged as a major industrialised state.

- Coal production doubled and that of iron and steel increased sevenfold from the 1890s to 1905.
- New technologies were introduced in the oil and chemical industries.

- The amount of railway track laid rose from 29,183 km in 1891 to 52,612 km in 1901. Much of this was facilitated by the considerable growth in capital investment from abroad, which increased on average 120 per cent every year from 1893 to 1898.
- Income from industry rose from 42 million roubles in 1893 to 161 million roubles by 1897.
- By 1900, Russian overtook France as the fourth largest iron producer in the world.

All of this, according to the historian Clive Trebilcock, led to an annual average rate of increase in industrial production of 7.5 per cent, 'far exceeding Russian achievement for any comparable period before 1914 and establishing one of the most impressive performances in late nineteenth-century Europe'.

However, it is easy to exaggerate Witte's influence on modernising the Russian economy.

- He focused on the development of heavy industry and neglected other industrial sectors, such as engineering and textiles. This was short-sighted as to an extent the demand for metals (and hence coal) came from other industries such as cotton textiles.
- The reliance on foreign capital has been criticised as dangerous. The loans could be recalled at short notice and reliance on foreign technological expertise stunted the emergence of home-grown talent.
- Although the railway system expanded considerably it was very costly and not as impressive as other parts of Europe. By 1914, Russia had 11 times fewer kilometres of track than Germany. Most railway investment was made in the Trans-Siberian line, which was started in 1892 (but never fully completed). Although this greatly aided the industrial and agricultural expansion of Siberia it was rushed and poorly constructed.
- Finally, Witte paid little attention to agriculture, which caused rural discontent and distrust among the government and was a major reason for his downfall in 1903.

Some believe that Witte's industrial programme was a dress rehearsal for Stalin's industrialisation of the 1930s (see pages 118–21). There are similarities but there was no distinct and logical progression from one to the other.

When Witte served as prime minister (1905–06), he influenced Nicholas II to adopt the October Manifesto and to end the war with Japan (see page 29). Both measures were viewed as necessary to stop the Russian government from collapsing. However, the more conservative members of government were wary of Witte and there is also an indication that Nicholas II thought the prime minister was attempting to meddle in affairs that were not his business. This is the main reason he was urged to resign in 1906.

Activity

1. Consider the following statements and using information from this section and further research find information to support and challenge the statements.
   - Witte's greatest achievement was as minister of finance.
   - Pobedonostsev's influence on Russia's government was limited.
   - Pobedonostsev had a greater influence on Russian government than Witte.
   - Witte was able to transform Russia's economy.
   - Pobedonostsev's conservative views ensured Russia's development was limited.
   - Russia was a major industrial state by 1905.
2. Which of these statements do you agree with the most? Explain your answer.

What was the importance of the Russo-Japanese War for Russia?

The decision made by Nicholas II to go to war with Japan in 1905 was based partly on the desire to strengthen Russia's world standing. It was also done to divert the population's attention from worsening economic and social conditions across the empire, particularly unemployment and underemployment, deteriorating working and living conditions, and inflation and food shortages. Thus, the overall intention was that the war

Vyacheslav Plevhe 1846-1904

Plevhe was a law graduate who joined the ministry of Justice and came to head the secret police He took a tough line against increasing terrorist activity and was a conservative monarchist. He was Minister of the Interior from 1902 and an adviser to the tsar. He supported war against Japan and was assassinated in 1904 by a socialist revolutionary.

A.N. Kuropatkin 1848–1925

Kuropatkin was a military reformer and war minister, 1898–1904.

V.N. Lamsdorff 1841–1907

Lamsdorff was one of Nicholas II's most valued ministers as foreign minister, 1900–05.

would help the governance of Russia. In practice, the reverse happened: the poor performance of the Russian military added to a sense of mistrust and lack of faith in the Russian leadership and helped fuel demands for wide-scale reforms.

Origins

Russia and Japan had long shown an interest in occupying and controlling Manchuria (in North Eastern China) and Korea. Since 1900, Russia had occupied parts of Manchuria, but in 1903, after a limited war with China, agreed to withdraw its forces. Some historians have argued that Japan was willing to work a trade-off that would have allowed Russia to stay in Manchuria while Japan took over Korea. However, it is unclear what the Russian government wanted. Some ministers, such as Plehve, minister for the interior, wanted an outright war with Japan to settle disagreements once and for all. This would have had the added bonus of deflecting the attention of the Russian public away from mounting domestic economic and social problems. Others including Kuropatkin and Lamsdorff, worried mainly about the financial cost and lack of preparedness were against war. There is more disagreement among historians over the stance of Witte. Witte questioned whether Russia could afford war. Japanese attempts at diplomacy over the Korean issue were rebuffed by the tsarist administration. Partly as a result, Japan, in 1902, formulated an alliance with Britain. As France was an ally of Britain, the French were unlikely to take sides with Russia if a war between Russia and Japan was to break out.

Russia did promise to withdraw troops from Manchuria but reneged on this which angered the Japanese. In February 1904, Japan retaliated by launching a night attack on the Russian Pacific Squadron at Port Arthur. Although something of a shambles, it resulted in damage to three Russian ships and appeared to dent Russian morale. Japan then proceeded to **blockade** Port Arthur. Preparations were made by both parties for a major sea battle.

Activity

1 Given the background to the Russo-Japanese War, draw up a balance sheet that shows what the likely costs and benefits would have been, as far as Russian officials including the Tsar were concerned, before making the decision to go to war? Use the table below to organise your comments.

Factors	Cost of going to war (hindrance)	Benefit of going to war (help)
Japan's interest in Korea		
Divisions within the ranks of Russian officials over relations with Japan		
Japan's alliance with Britain (and France)		
Russia's U-turn over Manchuria		

2 Do you think the Tsar's decision to go to war was correct? Explain your answer.

The course of the Russo-Japanese War: main events

- Battle of Yalu River (30 April–1 May 1904). The Japanese moved north from Korea to confront Russia in southern Manchuria. Outnumbered by about three to one, Russian forces were well beaten. This was an enormous shock to the tsar and the other Great Powers.
- The siege of Port Arthur continued, isolating about 60,000 Russian troops. In December 1905, the port eventually surrendered.
- In May 1905, Rozhestvensky's Baltic Squadron, on its way to relieve Port Arthur, came up against Admiral Togo's fleet at Tsushima Straits. This proved to be another terrible defeat for Russia and emphasised the technological superiority of the Japanese navy.
- In 1905, the final straw for Russia came with a humiliating defeat at Mukden. This prompted peace talks and the signing of a treaty.

The Treaty of Portsmouth, August 1905

The treaty that ended the war resulted in the following.

- Russia was forced to withdraw from Port Arthur, south Sakhalin and south Manchuria.
- Russian leaders had to acknowledge Japanese sovereignty in Korea.

◀ The course and end of the Russo-Japanese War and the countries involved

The impact of the war

The war revealed that Russian military leaders had a lack of knowledge, understanding and skill in dealing with an enemy that, on paper, was less powerful in military terms. The Russian public associated military incompetence with the tsar himself; this fuelled discontent at home rather than extinguished it, which had been one of the key aims of the war. It has even been argued that the social unrest that occurred in 1905 was tantamount to a revolution.

Reforms

Despite the expansion of Russia's rail network since the Crimean War (1853–56), the Russo-Japanese conflict revealed serious communication and transport weaknesses. The Trans-Siberian railway, still unfinished, had failed to solve the logistical problem of getting troops and supplies to war zones quickly and efficiently. The result was further investment in the transport infrastructure and industry. Ironically, such developments also led to rapid urbanisation and mounting public health problems. Poor working and living conditions produced an increasingly discontented populace; reforms enacted with the promise of raising living standards did the reverse (see page 33). However, there were many other influences on the outbreaks of unrest that occurred during 1905.

Activity

1 The Russo-Japanese War had a serious impact on Russia. Complete the table to help you assess the impact.

Factor	Impact	How serious was the impact
Prestige for Russia		
Economy		
Political		
Territorial		
Support for the Tsar		
Social		

2 In light of the information in your chart, plan an answer to the question 'Assess the impact of the Russo-Japanese War on Russia'.

Why was there a revolution in 1905?

The events of 1905 (see below) are said to have constituted a revolution as they led to a platform for political reform that in turn resulted, for the first time in Russia, in elections to a type of parliament called the *Duma*. The events can be seen to have arose from a mixture of economic, social, political and military influences. By 1905, critics of Nicholas II raised two main objections to his rule: the repressive nature of his government; and his inability to deal with political, economic and social problems, including the management of the Russo-Japanese war. Opposition had grown since the start of the twentieth century.

The opposition was characterised by the following.
- Growing support for political groups that were influenced by Populism and Marxism.
- The actions of the liberal intelligentsia led by Struve. Struve and fellow liberals wanted greater freedoms to be given to the people including the right to free speech, free worship and the right to vote. They were instrumental in getting Nicholas to agree to publish the October Manifesto (see page 33).
- Violence in the form of student unrest and the assassination of the minister of education, Nikolay Bogolepov (1901); strikes, such as that at the Obukhov factory in St Petersburg (1901); peasant protests linked to poor harvests (1902); anti-war protests leading to the assassination of the minister of the interior, Plehve (1904).

The trigger for intensified action, resembling a revolution, was Bloody Sunday, 9 January 1905.

What events appeared to cause a revolution?

The main 'revolutionary' events of 1905 were as follows.

Putilov strike

On 2 January 1905, about 12,000 workers from the Putilov steel works in St Petersburg went on strike. The strike was over the sacking of four workers for joining a kind of trade union known as the Assembly (trade unions were illegal). Other workers in St Petersburg came out in sympathy but throughout the rest of the Russian Empire there was limited evidence of industrial unrest. Strikes, such as the one at Putilov, were relatively common (although illegal), and were usually designed to achieve a specific aim such as higher wages or better working conditions. The intention was not to overthrow the existing political system and therefore it was not revolutionary in nature. Therefore, the Putilov strike did not seem to suggest the start of a revolution.

Bloody Sunday

The Putilov workers were part of a larger group that met on 9 January 1905 to march on the tsar's Winter Palace to present a petition demanding an eight-hour day, freedom of speech and an elected assembly. The petitioners were led by the political activist and priest, Father Gapon. When the group of about 150,000 strong arrived at Palace Square it was realised that the tsar was not in attendance; chaos ensued. Armed infantry, rather than the usual cavalry or Cossacks, were deployed to control the crowd. They fired upon the protesters killing over 200 people and injuring many more. The massacre was termed Bloody Sunday and had a unifying effect on individuals and groups who wanted to carry out further protests.

> **Father Georgy Gapon 1870–1906**
>
> Gapon was from a Ukrainian Cossack family. He became a government official and then entered the Russian Orthodox priesthood. He studied theology in St Petersburg and tried to help the factory workers. He was involved with a state-sponsored workers organisations and had links with the *Okhrana*. He led the procession of workers to the royal palace in January 1905, which led to Bloody Sunday. Afterwards he escaped to London. He was killed while trying to recruit fellow revolutionaries in Russia to be police spies.

◀ A painting of Bloody Sunday, 22 January 1905, produced shortly after the event

Events of February

The assassination of Grand Duke Sergei by members of the SR on 4 February should have sparked a massive clamp down on dissenters but instead it helped, along with more social unrest, to push the tsar to promise political reform. A consultative assembly, later to be called the *Duma*, was proposed, thus addressing the demands of Father Gapon and workers who were present on Bloody Sunday. More immediate measures were taken to relax restrictions on universities, to try to reduce agitation and unrest among students as the institutions had become hotbeds of radical activists. By the spring of 1905, St Petersburg university restrictions were lifted that had previously prevented professors and students from holding political meetings. The promises of reform and relaxation of restrictions on universities bought the government time to plan an effective response to opposition.

Establishment of unions

The government actions of February 1905 also provided the opposition with time to organise. In May, Paul Milyukov formed a Union of Unions, which was complemented in the following month by the All-Russian Peasant Union. Both put further pressure on the tsar.

Union of Unions

This was a group of leaders representing professionals, workers and the *zemstva*. Disillusioned with the slow progress being made by Nicholas II over political reforms and prompted by the naval disaster at Tsushima (see page 29), the Union of Unions demanded the setting up of a democratically elected constituent assembly.

All-Russian Peasant Union

In July 1905, peasants became politically organised for the first time with the founding of the All-Russian Peasants Union, which held its first meeting in Moscow. Their aims were similar to those of the Union of Unions but with the addition of a demand for land reforms. Peasant leaders wanted redistribution of land from the nobility to peasants on a much greater scale and in a more equitable fashion. This put the tsar under further pressure although the land issue remained unresolved until his fall in 1917.

Military mutinies

Without the support of the Russian army and navy, Nicholas II would not have survived as leader. Therefore, when the sailors of the battleship *Potemkin*, based in the Black Sea, mutinied in the summer of 1905 it alarmed the government. It was feared that it would lead to further mutinies and that, at a time when Russia was still at war with Japan, the government would collapse. Fortunately for the tsar, the *Potemkin* failed to engender support and sailed off hoping to find refuge in a remote part of the empire.

Battleship Potemkin

Potemkin was a tsarist warship whose crew mutinied when the ship was in port in Odessa in 1905. Forces were sent against the mutineers, but they got support from the sailors of other ships who refused to fire on the *Potemkin*, which was able to escape to Romania where the crew were given asylum. The ship was handed back to Russia after its crew had tried unsuccessfully to sink it. It was renamed and fought in the First World War, being finally scrapped by the USSR in 1923.

Establishment of the St Petersburg Soviet

In September 1905, another wave of strikes ensued, culminating in a general strike in October. On this occasion, workers attempted to coordinate their activities more effectively by forming soviets or workers councils. The largest soviets were established in St Petersburg and Moscow, and initially focused on campaigning for improved wages, shorter working hours and better working conditions. It was not long, though, before the revolutionary potential of the soviets was recognised by radicals, especially those from the SD and SR (see pages 19–20). Leon Trotsky (see pages 63–64) became chairman of the St Petersburg soviet and was instrumental in encouraging strike action to continue. The soviets were undoubtedly a major influence on Nicholas II's decision to call upon his ministers to formulate a manifesto for change and for this to be implemented as soon as possible.

The October Manifesto

Mainly in response to mounting opposition from liberals as well as workers and peasant organisations, Nicholas II was advised by Witte to issue a new declaration of his policy, or manifesto. The October Manifesto was an attempt to clarify the powers that a new legislative assembly might have. The proposals of the Manifesto were quite revolutionary as Russia seemed to be abandoning autocracy and moving towards a Western-style constitutional monarchy. The liberals, led by Milyukov and Struve, were appeased at least until they could see how the Manifesto would be put into operation. Workers and peasants were less impressed for, although the Manifesto promised greater freedoms, it was not obvious that their more immediate concerns were being addressed. Unsurprisingly, the end of 1905 witnessed further social unrest.

Events of November and December

In November 1905, another general strike occurred in St Petersburg, prompted and supported by the soviet. The strike merged into a more general rebellion, led by Bolshevik agitators from the soviet and lasted for five days. The rioting was put down by troops and the headquarters of the soviet closed. A similar, but larger uprising occurred in Moscow between 7 to 18 December. It prompted the authorities to use even more force, in the form of artillery, than they had done in St Petersburg. The result was a bloodbath; over 1000 people died and soviet properties were burnt to the ground. There was also rural unrest but peasants were somewhat fobbed off with a promise, in November, to reduce and eventually abolish redemption (mortgage) repayments on their land.

The causes

A range of economic, social, political and military factors can be seen to have caused the events of 1905.

Economic

Attempts to industrialise had resulted in some economic growth but workers did not appear to be reaping any benefits. Instead, they were suffering from poor working conditions, low pay, long hours and poor living conditions, especially the quality of housing, sanitation and water supplies. Workers responded by challenging employers and the government through striking and, later in the year, rioting.

Social

The considerable increase in the size of the population coupled with a backward agricultural sector meant many Russian people were always on the verge of starvation. This was worsened by a shortage of quality land for peasants to live and work on. Peasant unrest, especially later in 1905, contributed to the decision to make political reforms.

Political

The government increasingly faced political challenges from below, with the formation of pressure groups, such as the soviets and the All Russian Union of Peasants, and from above, especially in the form of the liberal intelligentsia, but also the middle class. The formation of a *Duma* was an obvious response to the demands from liberals for a more democratic political system (see page 18).

> **The October Manifesto**
>
> The manifesto stated that the assembly, or legislative *Duma* as it was called, would consist of elected representatives from the 51 provinces of the empire. The *Duma* would require the legalisation of political parties and trades unions. The assembly would provide the Russian people with freedom of speech, assembly and worship, which they did not previously have.

Military

The poor performance of the Russian military in the Russo-Japanese War added to the discontent caused by worsening economic and social conditions. A sense of patriotism was lost and many soldiers and sailors, who were recruited from the peasant and working classes, became so angry that they mutinied. This threatened the stability of the Russian government.

No one factor can be said to have caused the 1905 Revolution. The Revolution arose from the combination of a range of factors in a relatively short time and led to the October Manifesto and the formation of a *Duma*.

Activity

The crucial issues to understand are why there was a revolution in 1905 and the relative importance of the factors that brought it about.

1 Re-read this section and then complete the table below.

Factor	Explanation of the factor in causing the Revolution	Mark out of six for importance: 0 = not important; 6 = very important	Judgement

2 In light of the information in your table, what do you think was the most important cause of the 1905 Revolution? Explain your answer.

Was the 1905 Revolution a revolution?

A basic definition of political revolution is that it is the overthrow of a government by force in favour of a new political system. Such an overthrow, of course, would constitute dramatic and far-reaching change. When the events of 1905 are matched against this definition then no revolution occurred: it was simply a time of heightened social arrest. However, the historian and political scientist, Hannah Arendt, argued that a 'softer' view of revolution can be taken: it might be more appropriate to view it as a 'spontaneous, popular upheaval during which new forms of self-government were developed from below'. When this is applied to the events of 1905, then at least the platform for 'dramatic and far reaching change' would appear to have been laid.

What were the consequences of the 1905 Revolution?

The events of 1905 led to political reforms that at face value appeared revolutionary. The reforms were as follows.

- Rather reluctantly, Nicholas II introduced an element of democracy to Russia by setting up, in October 1905, the *Duma*. The hope was that the public would be convinced that the tsar was willing to become more accountable. It is unlikely that this would have happened without the war, as the tsar was a staunch adherent of 'autocracy, orthodoxy and nationalism'. This argument is reinforced by the fact that in a very short space of time the powers of the *Duma* were greatly diminished by the issuing of a set of Fundamental Laws.
- The October Manifesto satisfied the concerns of liberals, but only temporarily. In April 1906, Nicholas II announced the Fundamental Laws that stated that: 'The Sovereign Emperor possesses the initiative in all legislative matters. No law can come into force without his approval.' In other words, Nicholas was determined to keep control of how the legislative *Duma* was to go about its work.

- The creation of a *Duma* was accompanied by the introduction of a **franchise**. The vote was given to all men over the age of 25, but not to women or members of the armed forces. However, there was a weakness in the system as electoral districts within provinces were not equally represented.
- Between 1905 and Nicholas II's abdication in March 1917, four *Dumas* were called.

How did the four *Dumas* progress?

The *Dumas* that were allowed to meet had rather mixed fortunes.

First *Duma*, April–July 1906

Members of the first assembly participated in rigorous debate over matters of the Empire, such as the **Polish question**. However, the most important discussions concerned land distribution. The government stated that compulsory redistribution was not an option. This angered the First *Duma* who wanted a more radical solution; their disappointment and demands quickly gained press coverage. In response, Nicholas II claimed the actions of the *Duma* were illegal, and disbanded it after two months.

Between the sitting of the First and Second *Dumas*, a new approach to dealing with dissidents was adopted, sparked by the arrest, trial and imprisonment of key Kadet and **Labourist Party** members who had signed the **Vyborg Manifesto**. The new chairman of the Council of Ministers, Stolypin, thought that the process of dealing with dissenters was too cumbersome and 'soft'. He therefore ordered the trial system for civilian rioters to be accelerated by introducing field court-martials that resulted in fast trials and thousands of executions.

Second *Duma*, February–June 1907

The composition of the Second *Duma* was greatly affected by Stolypin's policies. There were fewer Kadets and Labourists, but more representatives from the SD, SR, Octobrists and the far right. However, the tsar and Stolypin continued to mistrust the work of the *Duma* over land reform and the management of the Russian army. When a SD member of the *Duma* was framed by the tsar for attempting to arrange an army mutiny, the tsar proclaimed that the *Duma* was subversive, dissolved it and overhauled the electoral system.

Third *Duma*, November 1907–June 1912

As a result of the electoral reforms, the Third *Duma* consisted mainly of people loyal to the crown, such as wealthy property owners from the countryside and cities. There was also a significant reduction in nationalist members from non-Russian parts of the empire. However, as the historian J.N. Westwood has pointed out, 'an unrepresentative *Duma* was not necessarily an ineffective *Duma*'. During the period, major reforms strengthened the army and navy. The judicial system was further improved with the reinstatement of justices of the peace and the abolition of land captains. For the first time, state-run insurance schemes for workers were introduced. All of this occurred because Nicholas II and his ministers showed more trust in the lower chamber. Even though Stolypin did his best to destabilise the *Duma* by manipulating Article 87 to create an even greater bias towards autocracy, the lower chamber served its full term of office.

> **Electoral reforms**
>
> These reforms were introduced by Stolypin in June 1907 and involved changes to the voting system. As a result: the wealthiest 1 per cent of the electorate controlled 66 per cent of all seats in the new duma; the representation for workers and peasants was cut by roughly one-half; non-Russian representation was slashed by over one-half.

> **Article 87**
>
> A section of the 1906 Fundamental Laws that allowed for proposed legislation to be submitted directly to the tsar for his approval without it having to be agreed to by the new *Duma*.

Russia 1894–1941

> **Lena Goldfields strike of 1912**
>
> At the end of February 1912, gold miners at the Lenzoto Gold Company in eastern Siberia complained about meat they had received at the company kitchen. Their complaints were ignored so they started a month-long strike that ended in the most notorious example of anti-worker violence during the reign of Nicholas II. The employers pleaded to the authorities to break up the strike, which only strengthened the resolve of the miners. On 4 April, matters came to a head; troops were sent to disband the strikers and resorted to firing upon those gathered. The Lena Goldfields Massacre, as it became known, resulted in between 200 and 300 worker deaths and as many as 400 to 500 non-fatal injuries. Solidarity strikes followed culminating in the general strike of July 1914.

Fourth *Duma*, November 1912–February 1917

The final *Duma* was again dominated by politicians from the far right. Its rule coincided with the brutal repression of civil disorder, such as when the state police killed striking miners at the Lena Goldfields (1912). This outraged many *Duma* members. It became infamous for putting pressure on the tsar to abdicate. Its members subsequently formed the backbone of the short-lived Provisional Government (see page 55). However, despite its criticism of the tsarist regime, the *Duma* remained an institution dominated by the 'old guard' of landowning conservatives and liberals.

Overall, it is clear that the *Duma* played an important role in instigating political, economic and social changes beneficial to many sectors of Russian society. Nevertheless, as historian Peter Waldron argues, collectively, the *Dumas* and the Council of Ministers 'made very little difference to the underlying nature of the Russian state'. *Duma* politicians on the left were largely ignored by the government, and the majority in the lower chamber remained loyal to the principle of autocracy.

The consequences of the events of 1905 can be viewed in two ways.

- In the short term, pressure from below seemed to result in concessions being made with the setting up of a Russian parliament (*Duma*).
- In the long term, the consequences may be seen to have been more dramatic: the *Duma* was seen to fail to meet the needs of those who expected more genuine and widespread political representation.

It is possible that 1905 was a 'dress rehearsal' for the revolutions of 1917. However, subsequent developments from 1905 to 1917 make it difficult to make a judgement about the importance of 1905 in leading to the abdication of the tsar and the coming of a communist regime.

> **Activity**
>
> One of the major results of the 1905 Revolution was the decision to establish *Dumas*. There has been much debate about their success.
> 1. Use the information in this section and further research to help you answer the following question, 'How successful were the Dumas in tackling the problems in Russia?'
> 2. Complete the following table to help you.
>
> | | Evidence of success | Evidence of failure | Judgement |
> |---|---|---|---|
> | First Duma | | | |
> | Second Duma | | | |
> | Third Duma | | | |
> | Fourth Duma | | | |

How successful were Stolypin's policies?

Stolypin's policies from 1905 to 1907 were partly a reaction to the social unrest that had materialised in 1905. Stolypin wanted to avoid a repeat of those events and used a mixture of reform and repression to achieve his aims.

Reforms: land redistribution

Rural unrest peaked during the years 1905–07. Stolypin, appointed as prime minister in 1906, looked to revamp government policy over land distribution. Stolypin's aim was to use land redistribution to build and strengthen the class of more able, educated and 'best' peasants (also referred to as *kulaks*). The hope was that they would then act as a role model for other peasants to follow as well as act as a force against the *mir*. To this end, the Stolypin reform (or 'wager on the strong') involved the following.

- Unused or poorly utilised land was made available to the Peasant Land Bank (established in 1883). Forward-looking peasants could then buy the land from the bank on favourable terms.
- Peasants who were still farming strips (small plots spread over two to three fields), under the instructions and authority of the *mir*, were given the right to consolidate their land into smallholdings. Hereditary household plots were not affected by this and it was also stipulated that land could not be immediately sold on to non-peasants. These provisos were designed to ensure that the mainstay of the Russian rural economy became the small peasant farm run independently by peasants.

In reality, the plan backfired because of the following reasons.

- The process led to an expansion in the numbers joining the wealthier class of peasants who in theory would be more loyal to the tsar. However, they were not totally satisfied with the reform, as they believed that the best land was still inaccessible to peasants.
- By 1914, about 2 million peasants left the village communes, leaving some regions very short of labour. The First World War accelerated this trend. This exodus added to the challenge of keeping supplies of food going to support the growing urban population.

> **'Wager on the Strong'**
>
> 'Wager' refers to Stolypin's hope that his reforms would create a group of prosperous landowners who would work independently of the *mir* and whose new acquisition of wealth would turn them into avid supporters of the tsarist regime. 'Strong' refers to the most mentally and physically able peasant farmers.

Repression – Stolypin's neckties

It was Stolypin who was responsible for the introduction of field court-martials in 1906 for civilian rioters (see page 35). The result was a series of very quick trials and executions, which gained the inglorious label of 'Stolypin's neckties' after the noose that was used in the hangings.

Table 2 The number of victims of terrorist activity (a) and the number of death sentences handed out to terrorists (b)

Year	Killed (a)	Wounded (a)	Sentenced (b)	Executed (b)
1905	233	358	72	10
1906	768	820	450	144
1907	1231	1312	1056	456
1908	394	615	1741	825

Source: Peter Oxley, *Russia 1855–1991*, page 72.

> **Activity**
>
> This section has considered the work of Peter Stolypin and it is important that you have a clear view about how successful his work was.
> 1 Use the information in this section and from further research to find evidence to either support or challenge the following statements.
>   - Stolypin's land reform policies had little success.
>   - It was only the outbreak of the First World War that prevented Stolypin's policies from bringing success.
>   - Stolypin's rule was brutal and harsh.
> 2 Which of these statements do you agree with most? Explain your answer.
> 3 In light of this, write one sentence that summarises Stolypin's career.

How far had the political, economic and social situation in Russia improved by 1914?

There was little reason in 1914 to believe that within three years, tsarism would have ended. In 1913, Russians celebrated the tercentenary of the Romanov dynasty; the populace were supportive of the tsar to a degree not witnessed for some time. Nicholas II had indeed survived a number of challenges to his authority and seemed to be in a strong enough position to cope with the challenges of the First World War.

The political situation in Russia in 1914

Politically, Russia was relatively stable. The creation of the *Duma* had initially caused Nicholas II some difficulties, as participants in the new assembly took the opportunity to criticise tsarist policies. But the tsar, with the help of Stolypin, reduced the authority of the *Dumas* and the challenge it posed faded. The liberal members of the *Duma* were aggrieved by what happened, but did not feel it was correct openly to defy the tsar. The more radical groups in 1914 still lacked enough support to consider mounting a revolution and, besides, many of their leaders, such as Lenin, had once more been exiled.

The economic condition of Russia in 1914

From 1909 to 1914, the economy, as measured by its **gross national product** (GNP), had grown at an average annual rate of 3.5 per cent, although this was still sluggish when compared with that of Russia's European rivals. There were also still low levels of industrial productivity. Factories employed vast amounts of labour to compensate for a lack of investment in modern technology. Many workers continued to be employed in small-scale handicraft enterprise. However, agricultural production had increased and Stolypin's 'wager on the strong' had resulted in the number of peasant households becoming independent farms rising from over 42,000 in 1907 to 134,500 in 1913. However, by 1914, the figure had fallen to just under 98,000, suggesting peasants had started to leave the land for urbanised areas. Russia's railway system had continued to develop so that by 1914, 70,160 kilometres of track existed (compared with 21,230 kilometres in 1881). However, the Trans-Siberian Railway had yet to be completed and thus parts of Russia were still unconnected to the 'centre'.

The state of Russian society in 1914

From 1897 (the time of the first census) to 1914, the population of Russia increased from 125 million to 166 million. This put pressure on those working on the land to increase the supply of food. Urbanisation had occurred at a rapid pace, although about 80 per cent of the Russian population still lived in rural areas. Nicholas II had paid little attention to the working and living conditions of those in towns and cities. In 1914, there were just over 1000 towns but only about 200 had piped water and just 38 had a sewerage system. Even after improvements, disease continued to spread. An outbreak of cholera in St Petersburg in 1910 caused over 100,000 deaths. Rising inflation, static wage levels and poor working conditions fuelled urban discontent. Economic and social changes had resulted in rising working-class consciousness and the potential for a challenge to tsarist authority from below. For example, the Lena Goldfields strike of 1912 was considered such a threat that the state sanctioned the killing of striking miners by troops.

Activity

1 Use the information in this section to assess how far the situation in Russia had improved by 1914. This will also help you understand the debate about the growth of stability in the period from 1905 to 1914. Complete the table below.

Factor	Evidence of improvement	Evidence that the situation had not improved	How far had it improved (mark out of six: 0 = no improvement; 6 = great improvement	Judgement on improvement
Political				
Economic				
Social				

2 Use the information from the table to help you plan an answer to the question, 'To what extent had the government addressed the problems Russia faced by 1914?'

Historical debate

How stable was Russia by 1914?

There is much disagreement among historians as to whether revolution was inevitable by mid-1914. Some regard the period from 1905 to 1914 as a period of stabilisation that was ended only by events at Sarajevo in 1914, suggesting that if this had not happened there would not have been revolutions in 1917. However, others have seen a revolutionary upsurge, particularly with industrial unrest in the period after 1912.

Read the following passages about the conditions in Russia in the period after 1905.

Passage 1

The general decline in rural disturbances after 1907 suggested to some observers that Stolypin had successfully diverted the peasantry from their quest for noble land through his land reforms. Yet the view that the reform was jeopardised only by the outbreak of war in 1914 no longer seems tenable. Applications to leave the commune declined long before the war began. The relative tranquillity of the countryside in the period before 1914 owed little to social change or technical improvement in the village. It is to be explained more in terms of a rapid increase in the amount of land sown, the recovery of grain prices, and a series of excellent harvests.

E. Acton, *Russia*, 1986

Passage 2

Wages in industry rose, but barely kept up with living costs, and the workday remained long, an average of ten hours on 1913. Housing conditions in the industrial centres deteriorated with the dramatic increase in the workforce by about a third between 1910 and 1914. In the working-class district of Moscow the average apartment accommodated nine persons in 1912, and four couples were crowded into one room of a model barracks at one factory. In St Petersburg the number of factory workers grew from 158,000 in 1908 to 216,000 in 1913. Many of them were fresh arrivals from the villages whose frustration at finding again the privations they had hoped to leave behind made them particularly prone to violence.

Hans Rogger, *Russia in the Age of Modernisation and Revolution*, 1983

Activity

1 Outline the arguments put forward in the two passages.
2 How far do the passages support the view that the period was one of stability?
3 How does Passage 1 support the view that the period was one of calm in the countryside?
4 What is there in the two passages to support the view that Russia was on the verge of revolution by 1914?
5 Using information from this chapter and from further research, which view do you most agree with?
  - The period from 1905 to 1914 was one of stability.
  - The period from 1905 to 1914 was one of strife.
  Explain your answer.

Further Research

Anna Geifman (ed.), *Russia Under the last Tsar: Opposition and Subversion 1894–1917*, Blackwell, 1999

Dominic Lieven, *Nicholas II: Emperor of All the Russia's*, Pimlico, 1993

Dominic Lieven, *Towards the Flame: Empire, War and the End of Tsarist Russia*, Allen Lane, 2015

Richard Pipes, *Russia Under the Old Regime*, Penguin, 1995

Robert Service, *The Last of the Tsars: Nicholas II and the Russian Revolution*, Macmillan, 2017

Ian D. Thatcher (ed.), *Late Imperial Russia Problems and Perspectives*, Manchester University Press, 2005

Ian D. Thatcher (ed.), *Regime and Society in Twentieth-Century Russia*, Macmillan, 1999

Chapter takeaways

- When Nicholas II came to the throne in 1894 he did not appear to have the character, ability and appropriate attitude to enable him to rule successfully. He appeared aloof, arrogant and lacking in intellect. This was borne out by much of his decision making up to the end of his reign in 1917.
- Nicholas faced a range of economic, social and political problems at the start of his reign. Most of these were linked either to the reactionary policies of his father or were even more deep rooted such as the land distribution issue that dated to the middle of the century.
- Opposition towards Nicholas II gathered momentum throughout his period on the throne. It came mainly from political parties and pressure groups of different political persuasions (liberals, socialists and Marxists). It was organised opposition that had a great deal to do with the end of the Romanov dynasty in 1917.
- National and religious minorities also caused Nicholas problems. Again, this issue had been inherited by the tsar but, nevertheless Nicholas struggled to fend off the demands for autonomy that arose from the minorities. In the case of Jews, he worsened the situation by continuing with pogroms.
- Nicholas was aided during his reign, to a greater or lesser extent, by able ministers, particularly Pobedonostsev, Witte and Stolypin. Any economic and political progress that was made was largely due to these individuals (especially Witte and Stolypin).
- Russia's involvement in the Russo-Japanese War proved to be a military disaster. The Russian army and navy suffered significant defeats and losses, which had a damaging impact on the morale of Russian people.
- The Russo-Japanese War coincided with a period of social unrest culminating in important political reforms. The unrest and reforms, often labelled a revolution, were caused by a range of economic, social and political factors that intertwined.
- The reforms that emerged from the 1905 Revolution came in the form of a manifesto for political change and the introduction of a democratically elected parliament called the *Duma*. However, the powers of the *Dumas* were restricted by the passing of Fundamental Laws, which were designed to protect the tsarist autocracy.
- There is some evidence to suggest that by 1914, the start of the First World War, the Russian economy, society and politics were in a fairly stable situation. There had been much social unrest and his authority had been challenged but he had survived this. There was little to suggest that within three years the Romanov dynasty would be finished.

Study skills: Understanding the wording of the question and planning an answer

The types of question set for AS and A level essays will be the same and therefore all the advice in this section applies to both examinations.

Understanding the wording of a question

It is very important that you read the wording of the question you are answering very carefully. You must focus on the key words and phrases in the question; these may be dates, ministers' names or phrases such as 'how successful'. Unless you directly address the demands of the question you will not score highly.

The first thing to do is to identify the command words; these will give you the instructions about what you have to do. You may be asked:

- to **assess** the causes of an event
- to **what extent**, or **how far** a particular factor was the most important in bringing about an event
- **how successful** a government or minister was.

Here are two example questions:

> **Examples**
>
> 1 **Assess the reasons for the 1905 Revolution.**
>
> In this essay, you would need to analyse a range of reasons why the Revolution of 1905 took place. However, in order to reach the highest levels you would need to weigh up – **assess** – the relative importance of the factors you have discussed and reach a balanced conclusion, not simply produce a list of reasons for the revolution.
>
> 2 **'The most important reason for the 1905 Revolution was Bloody Sunday.' How far do you agree?**
>
> Although this question, like the first, requires you to consider the reasons for the 1905 Revolution, you must consider the relative importance of Bloody Sunday and write a paragraph on the named factor, even if you argue it was not the most important. However, even if you think it was the most important, you must still explain why other factors were less important.

Planning an answer

Once you have understood the demands of the question, the next step is planning the answer. The plan should outline your line of argument – this means that you will need to think about your thesis before you start writing and the plan should help you maintain a consistent line of argument throughout the answer. Consequently, your plan should be a list of ideas and reasons relating to the issue in the question. Your plan should not be a date list of events, as this will encourage you to write a narrative or descriptive answer, rather than an analytical one.

Consider the first example above: 'Assess the reasons for the 1905 Revolution.'

A plan for this essay might take the following form:

> 1 **Economic reasons**
>   Low wages, long hours of work and poor working conditions led to waves of strikes throughout 1905. Strikes were organised later in the year by soviets and also under the influence of Bolshevik revolutionaries; this threatened political stability and partly caused Witte and Nicholas II to issue the October Manifesto. However, worker protests were ruthlessly suppressed (suggesting the authorities were less concerned about pressure from below for reform). Land issues also caused peasants to revolt although they were appeased by mortgage reforms.
>
> 2 **Social reasons**
>   Living conditions in cities and the countryside were poor; housing and sanitation was substandard relative to what existed in the western world and ordinary Russians often suffered food shortages. This may have fuelled discontent but is difficult to measure.
>
> 3 **Political reasons**
>   Workers, peasants and sections of the liberal middle classes demanded political reforms; this was evident from Bloody Sunday onwards. The liberals, in particular, gained the attention of Witte and the tsar as they had more power to destabilise the government from within.
>
> 4 **Military reasons**
>   The Russo-Japanese War went badly and caused discontent in all sectors of Russian society. This was also linked with mutinies by soldiers and sailors; without their support the tsarist regime would have collapsed.
>
> 5 **Conclusion**
>   The reasons are linked, especially the economic and political issues. However, the liberal demands for democracy with the background threat of civil disturbance was probably the most important reason for the revolution.

Your answer should not just list the reasons, but offer a comment about their importance and the conclusion should offer a clear line of argument which has been supported in the previous paragraphs.

Planning an answer should help you focus on the actual question and not simply write about the topic. In the first question it is wrong to write all you know about the Revolution of 1905 and then fail to identify the links between the reasons as to why it happened. Under the pressure of time in the examination room it is easy to forget the importance of planning and just start writing, but that will usually result in essays that do not have a clear argument or that change their line of argument halfway through, making it far less convincing.

Question practice

The focus of this section has been on planning. Use the information in this chapter to plan answers to the following questions:
1 'Pobedonostsev had more influence on the development of Russian government than Witte.' How far do you agree?
2 Assess the impact of the reforms made by Stolypin.
3 'The Russo-Japanese War had a limited effect on domestic affairs in Russia.' How far do you agree?

Short answer essay question

Which of the following posed the biggest challenge to the authority of Nicholas II?
(i) Political parties
(ii) National minorities.

Explain your answer with reference to (i) and (ii).

The 1917 Revolutions

This chapter deals with the dramatic political upheavals of 1917, which started with the abdication of Tsar Nicholas II and ended with the Provisional Government and Constituent Assembly being disbanded by Lenin and the Bolsheviks. The causes, course and consequences of the events of 1917 are looked at in detail. It is important to view the events in the wider context of Russia's continued involvement in the First World War; it was this that was the most decisive factor in determining whether the fall of the Romanov dynasty was to result in a democratic or similarly authoritarian form of government. The most intriguing question for historians is why, given the relatively low level of support for the Bolsheviks as late as the start of September 1917 Lenin was able to assume power by the end of the year.

The chapter addresses a number of key questions.

- What was the impact of the First World War on Russia?
- Why was there growing opposition to tsardom?
- Why was there a revolution in March 1917?
- Why did the Provisional Government struggle to impose its authority?
- Why was there a revolution in October 1917?

This chapter will also explain how to write an introductory paragraph to an essay and avoid irrelevance. It will focus on ensuring that the opening paragraph addresses the demands of the question and clearly outlines the line of argument to be pursued throughout the rest of the essay, rather than writing generally or irrelevantly about the topic.

Timeline

1914	August–December 1917	Russia was at war with Austria-Hungary and Germany
1917	18 February	Strike at the Putilov Steel Works
	19 February	Bread rationing was introduced
	23 February	Marchers celebrating International Women's Day and workers from the Putilov plant combined to protest about poor working and living conditions
	25 February	General strike – workers fired on by troops
	27 February	The Petrograd Soviet was formed alongside the Provisional *Duma* Committee
	1 March	Soviet Order No. 1 was passed, which gave the Petrograd Soviet total control over the whole of the Russian military
	2 March	Nicholas II abdicated, formation of the Provisional Government
	3 April	Lenin returned to Petrograd
	4 April	Lenin issued his *April Theses*
	May	Guchkov resigned as war minister and was replaced by Kerensky

3–6 July	Period of social unrest instigated by the Bolsheviks ('July Days') led to Lenin's exile again
8 September	The Bolsheviks controlled the Petrograd Soviet, by the middle of September they also controlled the Moscow Soviet
7 October	Lenin returned from exile
23 October	Kerensky closed *Pravda* and *Izvestiya* (Bolshevik newspapers); a round-up of leading Bolsheviks was attempted
24 October	The Petrograd Soviet's Military Revolutionary Committee began to seize power under the command of Trotsky
26 October	Most members of the Provisional Government were arrested; Kerensky fled
27 October	The All-Russian Congress of Soviets (in sitting since 25 October) was informed by Lenin that the Bolsheviks had seized power
2 November	The Bolsheviks had total control of Moscow
December	Peace talks at Brest-Litovsk resulted in the signing, on 3 March 1918, of a peace treaty

Overview

In August 1914, the Russian government committed itself to the First World War against Austria-Hungary and Germany. This was to have severe political, economic, social and military repercussions. After a successful Russian invasion of the German province of East Prussia and a victory at Gumbinnen, there were disastrous defeats at Tannenberg and the Masurian Lakes and Russian forces were forced out of Germany. Russian military efforts ebbed and flowed but by the late summer of 1917 troops were generally in retreat; the most significant indicator that the war was going badly was the Russian withdrawal, in August 1917, from the strategically important port of Riga in Latvia. In March 1918, the then Bolshevik government signed a peace treaty with Germany allowing Russia to withdraw from the First World War (but only after making dramatic concessions over territory). The war had brought great human and financial cost for Russia. The Russian economy was in chaos as industry had been geared solely for Russia to win the war. Agricultural production had increased but much food was diverted to feeding soldiers. Other factors, such as disrupted transport networks (and hence food distribution systems), in conjunction with military food requisitioning meant that large sections of the population started to starve. Ordinary people were also hit by inflation; owing to disruption in trade, the relocation of industry and the difficulty in accessing food, prices rose substantially.

The Russian government did not appear to handle the demands of war very well; some within government and outside of it blamed the tsar's leadership. Questions were asked about why Russia had entered into the war in the first place, Nicholas's decision to take command of the army and also his role in allowing his wife Alexandra and her friend, Rasputin, to influence the governance of Russia. Criticism early on in the war from within the **Duma** (and later via the Progressive Bloc) became so disturbing for the tsar that, in August 1915, he suspended it. However, this was not enough to stop the pressure mounting for changes to be made to the way the war was being handled, and coupled with worsening economic conditions and mounting social unrest Nicholas II abdicated in March 1917.

From March to October 1917, Russia was ruled by a temporary or Provisional Government made up mostly of members of the abandoned *Duma*. Running parallel to this was the Petrograd Soviet, a workers' council formed to campaign for greater representation of its member's interests. After a short time, the Provisional Government and Soviet collaborated to form what was known as a dual authority. This was to cause the Provisional Government problems as its decision

Russia 1894–1941

making was kept closely in check by the demands of the Soviet. The new government also faced a range of other challenges including Russia's continuation of the First World War, a deteriorating economy and illegal land appropriation by peasants from the gentry. A change in leadership in the summer of 1917, with the appointment of Kerensky, failed to halt growing social instability. Political exiles, such as Lenin and Trotsky, returned to Russia to stoke unrest (such as with the July Days) but there was also discontent among military personnel prompting an attempted coup in August 1917 (the Kornilov Revolt). The Provisional Government failed to deal with the challenges it faced and was forced by the Soviet and **Bolsheviks** to disband. By November 1918, the Bolsheviks under Lenin's leadership announced that they were now in control of Russia.

Gavrilo Princip 1894–1918

Princip was a Bosnian who was educated in Sarajevo. He travelled to Serbia where he was helped by nationalists to undertake an assassination plot against the Austrian heir to the throne, Franz Ferdinand. The initial plan failed but an unlucky change of plan by the royal visitor allowed Princip to kill both Franz Ferdinand and his wife on 28 June. Too young to be executed at 19, he was imprisoned and died of tuberculosis in 1918.

Schlieffen Plan and Eastern Front

In order to avoid war on two fronts German military planners aimed to defeat France by a rapid campaign and then shift the bulk of the German forces to meet the large but poorly led Russian army. The plan failed in 1914, leaving the war to rage on two fronts – the Western Front in France and Belgium and the Eastern Front where Russia fought Germany and Austria-Hungary.

What was the impact of the First World War on Russia?

A common view is that the First World War was a disaster for Russia. It acted as a catalyst for the overthrow of the Romanov dynasty, and had a highly damaging impact on the living and working conditions of ordinary Russians.

From the perspective of those who claimed to be representing the interests of the working class, for example, the Bolsheviks, the war was seen not as a disaster but as an opportunity. The Russian Marxists argued that the war was an inevitable consequence of the world capitalist system spiralling out of control and that it gave them the chance to achieve a permanent revolution in Russia that would lead to improved lives for its inhabitants. Moreover, the war was not necessarily a disaster for some national minorities as both Finland and Poland used it as a vehicle to gain independence (see pages 23–4).

Why did Russia enter the First World War?

In June 1914, Archduke Franz Ferdinand of Austria-Hungary was assassinated by Gavrilo Princip, a member of a Serbian nationalist group. From this point in time it would have been difficult for Russia not to get involved in a disagreement that was likely to grow into a much bigger conflict. Russia had an obligation to protect Serbia, a fellow Slavic state, against possible Austrian retaliation. There was also the prospect that the incident would galvanise Austria-Hungary into using a war against Serbia as a springboard for making other gains in the Balkans, which would have been detrimental to Russian interests.

Russia mobilised on 30 July in the hope of deterring Germany and Austria-Hungary from acting, but it failed and was quickly followed by the implementation of the German **Schlieffen Plan** and further built on by the establishment of an **Eastern Front**. This rapid escalation of the conflict was what the bulk of Russian leaders had feared the most.

The course of the war

An outline of the course of the war from a Russian perspective gives some indication of the immediate impact it was likely to have on Russia in general.

> **August and September 1914**: An initial Russian victory at Gumbinnen, was followed by disastrous defeats at Tannenberg and the Masurian Lakes (all three in East Prussia).
>
> **October 1914**: The Ottoman Empire entered the war on Germany's side and attacked Russian ports. This forced Russia into fighting a third major power, in addition to Germany and Austria-Hungary, and into campaign in the Caucasus region.
>
> **February 1915**: Russian forces were pushed back from East Prussia but in March managed to take Memel.
>
> **August 1915**: Nicholas II took personal command of the Russian forces, much to the consternation of many of his advisers. The Russian retreat was temporarily halted but by September Nicholas was forced to abandon Vilnius.
>
> **February 1916**: A glimmer of hope emerged as Russian troops took Ezerum, in Turkey, from the Ottomans.
>
> **June 1916**: The Brusilov Offensive was launched with the intention of gaining lost ground and appeasing discontent that was spreading at home. There was some initial success but the Germans defeated the threat.
>
> **June and July 1917**: An all-out attack on Austrian forces was made but by the end of July the Russians were once more in retreat.
>
> **August 1917**: Russia withdrew from the strategically important port of Riga in Latvia.
>
> **December 1917**: Peace talks at Brest-Litovsk resulted in the signing of a treaty (1918). Trotsky claimed that the conditions amounted to a *diktat*.

The events of the course of the war are unambiguous. Russia did badly and much of this was blamed on poor military and political decision making.

The impact of the war

The war had consequences for military organisation, the economy (including communication infrastructures) and society. A useful way of interpreting these consequences is to compare the level of resilience of tsarism (the 'optimist view') against the underlying forces for change that had emerged before the war (the 'pessimist view').

Military organisation: defeats and material losses

Many military historians agree that the best chance of Russian military success was at the start of the war. However, the terrible defeats at Tannenberg and the Masurian Lakes meant that the morale of the Russian troops was severely dented. Russian soldiers had actually fought well but they were let down by the poor tactical decision making of their Generals Samsonov and Rennenkampf. The Russians lost twice as many troops as the enemy during these early campaigns and the hope at home that Russia would score an early victory with their sheer weight of numbers, often described as the 'Russian steamroller', waned. Russian casualties for the whole of the war were around 8 million, including 1.7 million dead and 2.4 million captured.

By the end of 1915, Stavka, the command centre for the Russian army, blamed lack of military progress on the 'shells crisis' (the lack of munitions reaching soldiers fighting on the frontlines). The implication of this was that industry was struggling to keep up with the demands of the army and, therefore, workers had to put much more effort into increasing munitions production. The truth of the matter was that industry was already working near to full capacity. As the historian Norman Stone has argued, the problem was not that there was a deficit of munitions, but it was more a case that military administrators did not have the ability to cope with the logistical challenges posed by the war. This was made worse by communication and transport problems (similar to those that existed in the Russo-Japanese War, see pages 29–30). It was not surprising that stockpiling of supplies occurred; piles of foodstuffs rotted away and, at Archangel (in northern Russia), the mountains of hardware were so great that they started to sink into the ground!

Further defeats and the subsequent Great Retreat in 1915 prompted Nicholas II to take the step of taking personal control of the armed forces. By early 1916, it looked as though Russian military prospects had picked up. However, the tsar's decision to leave the capital (now called Petrograd) left a political vacuum. The Tsarina, Alexandra, was left as a temporary *de facto* ruler. This was not popular with the *Duma* and supporters of the tsar, partly owing to Alexandra's German background but also because of her friendship with Rasputin (see pages 51–52). All of this resulted in mounting criticism of Nicholas and a window of opportunity for those who wanted to push for a more liberal political system.

Although Russia's war effort seemed to improve throughout 1916, the failure of the Brusilov offensive and the resort to **attritional warfare** gave the indication that the tsar was not capable of bringing the conflict to a satisfactory end. By the time the tsar was forced to abdicate, it was certain that Russia would be defeated by Germany. Nevertheless, the domestic upheaval that proceeded throughout 1917 meant that the war was unlikely to turn in Russia's favour and the Bolshevik decision to withdraw from the conflict in 1918 was, for many, sensible and logical. Not all agreed with this decision; patriots (mainly conservatives and supporters of the Tsar) and a host of others of various political persuasions wanted a continuation of the war to the bitter end.

> **Petrograd**
>
> St Petersburg was renamed Petrograd in August 1914 after the start of the war. The tsar ordered the renaming as he thought St Petersburg (Sankt-Petersburg) sounded German.

> **Brusilov offensive**
>
> General Alex Brusilov was Russia's most able military commander. He was noted for his strategic and tactical skill as well as for his genuine concern over the welfare of his troops. During the First World War he experienced early military successes on the south-western front and also in 1916. Brusilov planned a renewed attack on the south-western front. The aim was to catch the Austrian-Hungarian troops by surprise. On 4 June, the Brusilov offensive was launched and resulted in a headlong retreat of the enemy. The Austrian-Hungarian armies suffered heavy casualties; nearly 200,000 troops were killed and much of their equipment destroyed. The assault was so successful that the Russian leadership started to think that outright victory in the war was possible. However, Brusilov's efforts were not backed up by those of his fellow commanders elsewhere. Others, such as General Evert, were slow to act, the result being a state of attritional warfare on other parts of the fronts.

Tsar Nicholas II inspecting Brusilov's Infantry Division, 1916

Economic: dislocation and inflation

The financial burden of the war was huge, although this became apparent only from the middle of 1916 onwards. The total cost was in the region of 3 billion roubles, which far exceeded levels of government expenditure during peacetime. (In 1913, for example, government expenditure was about 1.5 billion roubles.) The cost was met partly through borrowing (foreign loans, war bonds), increases in tax (income, excess profits) and printing more money. Such measures worked to an extent; for most of the war, enough money was invested in Russian industry to enable it to meet the projected demands of the military. It also meant that Russian workers were fully employed and received a regular and slightly higher income than usual. However, the latter was offset by **rampant inflation**, the inevitable consequence of an increase in the circulation of money. Prices had risen 400 per cent by 1917 from the start of the war, with those on fixed incomes (the elderly and low paid, unskilled workers) suffering greatly.

For the optimists, adverse wartime conditions on such a scale had never existed before. It was not surprising that such unique circumstances united those who suffered the most hardship to challenge the ruling elite and demand a far more representative form of government.

Social: food shortages

Even if peasants and workers were able to maintain at least a decent level of real income, the likelihood of being able to spend it on even the bare necessities declined as the war progressed. This was especially the case after 1916 with food supplies. Throughout the war period, the average output of cereals was higher than it had been during the first decade of the twentieth century. But, a rapidly rising population, food requisitioning by the army, a fall in the availability of fertilisers and transport problems all worked together to create food shortages. Some historians have pointed out that this was largely a regional problem; those in Petrograd suffered more than

> **War bonds**
>
> Government savings certificates sold during wartime to the public with a promised fixed rate of return after the war. They had the important psychological impact of helping people feel that they were making a valid contribution to the war effort.

others, with, for example their bread ration falling 25 per cent in the first three months of 1916. But regional variation is not particularly important as the social unrest that resulted from high prices and shortages gathered momentum in the places where it was likely to have the greatest impact – the growing towns and cities in the west of Russia.

Transport and communications

The war placed severe pressures on the transport system in Russia, particularly the railways. Lines became blocked, signalling mechanisms broke down and engines became stranded (often as a result of running out of fuel). Railway stations and depots started to struggle to handle the vast volumes of freight (mainly munitions and food). As indicated in the sections above, all of this was to have serious repercussions for the supply of materials and food to soldiers and civilians.

Activity

There is much debate among historians about the role of the First World War in bringing about the fall of tsarism (see also the Historical debate section on pages 66–7).

1 Re-read this section and use the information to help you complete the table below that addresses the key question: 'The First World War was the main reason for the fall of Nicholas II.' How far do you agree? Write your ideas out in bullet point form.

The First World War was the main reason ...	There were other reasons ...

2 Complete the activity by colour coding what you think is the most to least important reasons: green for very, yellow for medium and red for minimal. Once done, write a summary answer, in up to four sentences, to the question.

Why was there growing opposition to tsardom?

In many ways Nicholas II was responsible for his own downfall in March 1917; his leadership during the First World War was poor and showed traits similar to those in evidence in the pre-war period.

- He ignored how the war affected the well-being of the Russian people on the home front. He seemed more interested in discussing, with his ministers, trivia rather than the pressing problem of food shortages.
- His decision to take command of the armed forces in August 1915 obviously backfired. Nicholas had some training as a soldier (in a cavalry regiment) but this did not prepare him for the demands of a conflict on the scale of the First World War. His views on strategy and tactics were unoriginal. He gave the impression that, when he based himself in the military headquarters at Mogilev, it was to take a holiday from the pressures that were mounting in Petrograd. For example, he would often request to go for a ride in his Rolls-Royce in the Russian countryside or to play dominoes when he should have been focusing on the war effort.
- Nicholas relied on generals who were of mixed calibre. The tsar made some good appointments (Brusilov, for example) but also some very poor ones (Kuropatkin, for example). This might not have been too big a problem

Alexei Brusilov 1853–1926

Brusilov was a skilled cavalry officer who fought in the war against Turkey 1877–78. He commanded a major offensive against Austria Hungary in 1916, which concentrated forces and used smaller well trained units. He is regarded as a highly successful and innovative commander by military historians

Alexei Kuropatkin 1848–1925

Kuropatkin, as minister of war, had opposed the war against Japan 1904. He commanded Russian forces poorly in Manchuria. He was recalled in 1915 and went on to mismanage the Northern Front through costly frontal assaults and a failure to support more imaginative commanders. He was sacked in 1916.

but Nicholas exacerbated matters by not consistently supporting his commanders and by allowing infighting between them to occur. Witte claimed Nicholas did not have the willpower to deal with key military figures and Rasputin went further by saying he did not have the courage to do so.

- His decision to act as chief of the army had serious repercussions for the governance of Russia more generally (see the sections on the influence of Alexandra and Rasputin below).

Alternatively, the fall of the tsar might be seen to have resulted from a mixture of circumstance, the incompetence and deviousness of others and bad luck.

- There was no obvious reason for Nicholas to have believed that the war would go as badly as it did; it should also be remembered that he was reluctant to enter the war in the first place, but in many ways he had little option.
- Nicholas made military appointments in good faith and probably did not bargain on the incompetency of some generals, such as Evert and Kuropatkin.
- Individuals, such as Rasputin, appeared determined to undermine the authority of the tsar.

Overall, it is possible to defend Nicholas's actions but he was still responsible for, with hindsight, some poor decision making especially when it came to the appointment and trust he placed in key military personnel.

Tsarina Alexandra's influence on Russian government

In 1894, Princess Alexandra married Nicholas II and subsequently took on the title of Empress of Russia (and Tsarina). Alexandra was the German granddaughter of Britain's Queen Victoria; both of these foreign connections caused suspicion among the Russian people. The empress had inherited the haemophilic gene from her grandmother and passed it on to her son Alexei. This was significant, as it was to influence her relationship with the religious mystic, Rasputin.

Alexandra was deeply religious and was quick to adopt the Russian Orthodox Church. Her faith influenced her attitude towards the royal court, which she thought was too ostentatious, and to peasants, with whom she sympathised.

From 1915, when he took control of the army, Nicholas II was away at the Eastern Front for much of the time. This left the governance of Russia in the hands of Alexandra and Rasputin, who by this time had become a personal adviser to the empress. The historian Orlando Figes has claimed Alexandra then became 'the real autocrat in the capital', although she was encouraged by her 'holy friend' who 'used her as a mouthpiece for his own pretensions to power'. In particular, Alexandra used her authority to appoint ministers whom she could manipulate and would not question her role from within the *Duma*. For example, she appointed and dismissed three ministers to the position of chairman of the Council of Ministers until she arrived at the one (Prince Nikolai Golitsyn) whom she deemed to be the most accommodating. On occasion her appointments were questioned, such as in the case of Alexander Protopopov who was given the post of minister of internal affairs, but Alexandra pleaded and demanded that they should be adhered to. This clearly indicates that her influence on Russian government was considerable and that she showed a level of determination and decisiveness that was not always displayed by her husband.

Alexandra's most significant political decision was the sacking, in March 1916, of Alex Polikanov, the minister of war. He was considered by fellow

Gregory Efimovich Rasputin 1871–1916

Rasputin was born in Western Siberia to a peasant family. He spent some time in an Orthodox monastery before travelling around Russia. In 1903, he arrived in St Petersburg and quickly gained a reputation as a mystical healer, but also as a sexual predator. In 1905, he had been introduced to the tsar and tsarina as someone who might be able to cure Alexei of his illness. After becoming acquainted with Rasputin, Alexei's health did seem to improve, which endeared the monk to Alexandra. In 1916, Rasputin was murdered, under strange circumstances, by a group of aristocrats.

Alexander Protopopov 1866–1918

Protopopov was from a wealthy noble family. A charming former cavalry officer he was appointed minister of the interior in 1916 and virtually ran Russia. Reactionary and incompetent he suppressed criticisms, failed to solve the food crisis and to foresee the revolution. Delusional, he was reduced to consulting the ghost of Rasputin. He was executed in 1918.

> **Progressive Bloc**
>
> In early 1915, the *Duma* asked Nicholas II to replace his cabinet, which they believed to be incompetent to deal with the war, with a 'ministry of national confidence'. It was argued that the new body should be made up of more forward-looking *Duma* members. Nicholas rejected the idea, which caused the proposers to form a group to persuade the tsar to adopt more progressive ideas. It consisted of Kadets, Octobrists and Progressists; they became known as the 'Progressive Bloc'.

politicians as one of the most able Russian administrators of all time but the tsarina claimed he sympathised with revolutionists. This kind of action caused much discontent within the government and was part of the reasons for the formation of a 'Progressive Bloc' in the *Duma* to put pressure on the tsar to take firmer control of proceedings.

Rasputin's influence on Russian government

If Rasputin had any influence on Russian government it came through his friendship with the tsarina. Through helping her son, Alexei, Rasputin won over the confidence and admiration of Alexandra. If Rasputin had wanted to help shape Russian political affairs then he would have done so by persuading Alexandra to making certain ministerial appointments or formulating a particular policy. However, there is little evidence to support this. The main indicator of his interference is when he was asked to reorganise the army's medical supply system. However, this hardly indicates that he wanted to shape the direction that Russian government was taking.

Nonetheless, he was obviously seen as having some negative level of influence over the royal family as he was despised by the tsar's advisers. It is possible that such ill-feeling was a result of envy; Rasputin does seem to have shown aptitude as an administrator (as in the case of dealing with the medical supplies issue).

The role of the Fourth *Duma*

When the final (fourth) *Duma* was called (November 1912–February 1917) it was once more dominated by politicians from the far right (ultra conservatives). Its tenure coincided with heightened and brutal repression of civil disorder. This was characterised by state police killing striking miners at the Lena Goldfields (1912) (see page 36). The murders outraged many *Duma* members who viewed this as a retrograde step by the government in its attempt to deal with Russia's economic and social problems. Guchkov (see page 19), leader of the moderate Octobrists, warned the tsar and ministers that the Russian people had become revolutionised by the actions of the government and that they had lost faith in its leaders. In 1914, the *Duma* made the following proclamation and prophecy of doom:

> The Ministry of the Interior systematically scorns public opinion and ignores the repeated wishes of the new legislature. The *Duma* considered it pointless to express any new wishes in regard to internal policy. The Ministry's activities arouse dissatisfaction among the broad masses that have hitherto been peaceful. Such a situation threatens Russia with untold dangers.
>
> Cited in Theofanis George Stavrou, *Russia Under the Last Czar*, 1969

The progress of the fourth *Duma* was interrupted by the outbreak of the First World War in 1914. The *Duma* met a week after the start of the war, but its work was disrupted when a group of socialist members walked out mainly at Nicholas II's decision to commit Russia to a war they considered unwinnable. However, initially the *Duma* had backed the tsar and voted for its own suspension for the duration of the war but in 1915, with the military failings it demanded its own recall and met for six weeks before it was prorogued following its demand for a national government to take charge of the war effort. Nicholas responded by suspending the *Duma* in August 1915, and personally taking charge of the armed forces.

This was the last chance he had of maintaining the support of the progressive parties. The result was that many members formed the 'Progressive Bloc', which criticised the management of the war and tried to persuade Nicholas to make concessions, but he continued to be unwilling to listen. As his government proved increasingly incapable of running the war so the *Duma* changed from being a supporter at the start of the war to an opponent. However, despite its criticisms of government rule, it remained an institution that was dominated by the 'old guard' (supporters of tsarism and authoritarian rule). The final *Duma* became infamous for eventually putting pressure on the tsar to abdicate in March 1917 and went on to form the backbone of the short-lived Provisional Government.

The decision by Nicholas to go to the front was criticised by many and, at least in part, this was because it left the unpopular tsarina and Rasputin in charge of affairs in Petrograd. As neither were trusted by Russia's elite this further weakened the position of Nicholas and was made worse by the deteriorating position both on the home front and in the war. Therefore, although Nicholas' decision might be seen as heroic and an attempt to strengthen Russia's position, it backfired and played a crucial role in his downfall.

Activity

This section has looked at the reasons for the growing opposition to tsardom.

1 Re-read the section and complete the following table to help you explain why there was growing opposition.

Issue	How did it create opposition?	How important was the issue in creating opposition (mark out of six: 0 = not important; 6 = very important)	Judgement
Actions and policies of Nicholas II			
The role of Alexandra			
The role of Rasputin			
Nicholas II attitude to the Fourth *Duma*			
The formation of the Progressive Bloc			
Nicholas decision to go to the front			

2 Using your completed table consider the question: 'How much opposition was there to the Tsar by 1917?' What was the significance of the opposition?

Why was there a revolution in March 1917?

Military weaknesses and mounting economic problems gave fuel to the critics of the tsar. The fact that the Brusilov Offensive had not led to an outright military victory appeared to dishearten and exhaust the tsar. Nevertheless, by early 1917 Nicholas II still thought that by spring another offensive would be possible and that '… God will give us victory, and moods will change'.

Within three months, though, he had abdicated. There were three main steps towards this revolutionary event.

Step 1: Unrest in Petrograd

There were mounting protests in Petrograd from January 1917 onwards. On 9 January 1917, about 150,000 workers took to the streets of St Petersburg to commemorate the anniversary of Bloody Sunday. A major strike occurred at the Putilov Steel Works on 18 February; strikers were joined by other workers who had heard rumours about further bread rationing (which was indeed introduced on 19 February). On 23 February, marchers celebrating International Women's Day and workers from the Putilov plant combined to protest about poor working and living conditions. All of this culminated in a general strike (25 February). On 26 February, the *Duma* defied an instruction from the tsar to disband, after making demands on him to form a national government to deal with the war. A major turning point was the decision by troops (about half of the Petrograd Garrison) to join the protesters. By the end of the month, the situation had become chaotic and uncontrollable.

Step 2: The Formation of the Petrograd Soviet

On 27 February, the Petrograd Soviet was formed alongside the Provisional *Duma* Committee. This was the foundation of governance through a dual authority and a clear indication that the tsar was considered unfit to rule by a majority of senior politicians. The potential potency of the Petrograd Soviet was illustrated by, on 1 March 1917, the issuing of Soviet Order No. 1. This gave the Soviet total control over the Russian military. With such weakened control over the armed forces it seemed impossible for the tsar to continue in office.

Step 3: Pressure on the Tsar to abdicate

Rodzianko, president of the *Duma*, had urged the tsar to 'change' his attitude towards governing. On hearing Rodzianko's pleas, Nicholas decided to return to Petrograd on 28 February in the hope that he could calm things down. However, on the way mutinous troops hijacked the royal train and diverted it to Pskov, 300 kilometres from Petrograd. Waiting there were members of the high command of the Russian army (*Stavka*) and the *Duma*. They told Nicholas he was wasting his time returning to Petrograd as he would probably be attacked and violently deposed. He was advised to abdicate immediately.

Although the pressure on Nicholas to abdicate must have been overwhelming he continued to procrastinate. He considered renouncing his throne and handing it over to his son before, on 2 March, officially giving in and nominating his brother, Grand Duke Michael, as his successor. But the Grand Duke refused claiming that without the backing of a constituent assembly of some kind, he would be doomed to fail. On 3 March, the Provisional Committee of the *Duma* formed a Provisional Government; Romanov rule had come to an end and a revolution in Russian government had taken place. Some commentators, though, claim this was more of a platform for the Bolshevik build-up of power culminating in the introduction of communism after October 1917.

Some historians have argued that the continuation of the war made it impossible for the temporary government to deal with the burning issues of land reform, the modernisation of industry and the call for a constituent assembly. Thus, the war gave an opportunity to revolutionaries to overthrow the government completely and install their own form of direct rule.

Formation of the Petrograd Soviet

The word Soviet means a council and in 1905 there had been councils of workers. The Soviet of 1917 originated in a Central Workers Group founded in 1915 by Menshevik socialists. Arrested in January 1917, they were freed by crowds in February and organised elections by workers and soldiers for a council to meet in the Tauride palace. By March this had grown to 3000 deputies and was an alternative authority to the *Duma*.

Grand Duke Michael 1878–1918

Michael was the younger brother of Nicholas II and heir in 1899 before the birth of Alexei, the tsarevich. Exiled because of a scandal over his marriage in 1912, he returned to command a cavalry regiment in 1914 and was named as successor by Nicholas II in March 1918. He did not accept but was imprisoned in August 1917 by the Provisional Government and killed by the Bolsheviks in 1918.

> **Activity**
>
> This section has focused on why the tsar abdicated in March 1917. In order to understand why this happened it might be helpful to compare the situation in March 1917 with that in 1905 and look at what was different.
>
> 1 In order to do this, you will need to re-read the section on 1905 in the previous chapter, see pages 30–4. Complete the following table to help you.
>
> | Factor | Situation in 1905 | Situation in 1917 |
> |---|---|---|
> | Performance in war | | |
> | Support of the army | | |
> | Economic problems | | |
> | Support of the ruling elite | | |
> | Opposition | | |
> | Attitude of the peasantry | | |
> | Food supplies | | |
>
> 2 Use the chart to help you consider what was different in 1917 to 1905.
> - Were any of the problems the same?
> - What had changed?
> - What do you think was the greatest difference for Nicholas? Explain why this may have forced him to abdicate?

Why did the Provisional Government struggle to impose its authority?

The formation and tenure of the Provisional Government has caused much debate among historians. One area of disagreement is the extent to which the government failed. Some believe that the Provisional Government was doomed from the start but did not help itself by making poor decisions. Others argue that the new government was successful in achieving its main aim, which was the preparation for elections to a new constituent assembly. Therefore, it was not so much the failings of the Provisional Government that led to the October revolution of 1917 but rather the determination of the Bolsheviks to seize power.

From March to September 1917, the Provisional Government struggled to impose its authority in the face of considerable opposition (especially from the 'left': Bolsheviks, **Mensheviks**, the SR and the soviets). A major reason for this was that the majority of members of other parties wanted a short-term government based on consensus, with the main aim of creating a constituent assembly. The leading Bolsheviks, though, rejected this since it would favour 'old interests' to the detriment of workers and peasants. To understand why the Bolsheviks in particular had little faith in the Provisional Government it is important to look at its background and composition.

Who were the members of the Provisional Government?

The origins of the Provisional Government can be dated to 1915. In that year, two-thirds of the *Duma* (mostly moderates) collaborated to form the Progressive Bloc. The aim was to create unity among different party members so that an agreed plan to manage Russia's war effort could be implemented. Nicholas II saw this as an affront to his authority and in August 1915 he ordered the *Duma* to be suspended. The result was increased discontent with the tsar from across the political spectrum. In February 1917, a series of strikes and demonstrations led to the fourth *Duma* dissolving itself. By the end of the month, the Winter Palace and other government buildings had been taken over by revolutionaries. Chaos ensued until a Temporary Committee, created from the leading figures in the last *Duma*, and a Provisional Executive of the Soviet of Workers' Deputies co-operated to formulate a programme for order to be restored.

On 1 March, the Tsar agreed to hand over authority to the Temporary Committee and, on 2 March, he abdicated. The new Provisional Government, as it was labelled, was immediately revealed to the Russian peoples. For those historians who view the Provisional Government as an abject failure much is made of the initial composition of its core members or Cabinet

Members

The historian J.N. Westwood, in *Endurance and Endeavour: Russian History 1812–2001* (2002), has claimed that the Provisional Government was initially 'popularly accepted'. Its members were, in the main, liberal minded and some, such as Milyukov and Guchkov, were well known political figures. Others, though, were more obscure characters. The majority were masons although the extent to which this may have caused consternation among the general public at the time is debateable; masons tended to meet in secret and their identities would be known only to fellow freemasons. Of more significance is the fact that the new government lacked legitimacy as it was an unelected body made up from members of the Progressive Bloc. This view is strengthened by the response of a member of a crowd that listened to Milyukov's announcement of the composition of the Provisional Government; 'Who appointed you?' was shouted out. Milyukov rather lamely responded by stating it was 'the Revolution itself'.

> **Freemasons**
>
> Members of a society of freemasons. Freemasons, going back to the Middle Ages, were said to be individuals with highly developed craft skills (such as stone masons, those who chiselled and crafted stones for building). Such workers formed secret societies to protect their income and their mutual interests.

Why did the Provisional Government struggle to govern effectively?

Some historians have argued that the era of the Provisional Government was the only time that the Russian Empire was united. Others have pointed out that it was unlikely that the new government would have been able to sustain unity. It faced the following challenges although most of these had grown over a long period of time.

Dealing with the war

There is debate among historians over the impact of the First World War on the Provisional Government. For some, the formation of the Provisional Government was not a disaster and it was not necessarily doomed to fail; it was the continuation of the war that meant the new regime struggled to establish its authority. If Russia had pulled out of the war in March 1917, it was possible that the Provisional Government would have succeeded with the added possibility of the reinstatement of the tsar to create a **constitutional monarchy**.

More specifically, some claim that the war hindered the progress of the Provisional Government for the following reasons.
- The war had popular support; demands for withdrawal and peace were made on the basis that this would be honourable and unconditional. It was unlikely Germany would agree to such a deal given the strong military position it was in by March 1917.

- The war was costly in terms of the impact on land, labour (especially soldiers) and capital. The Provisional Government also felt committed to continuing the war given that much had already been invested in trying to win it.
- The Provisional Government had limited support from its allies (Britain and France), who were desperate for Russia to stay in the war and put pressure on the Provisional Government not to countenance any idea about brokering a separate peace with Germany.
- Challenges, such as land distribution and the impact of urbanisation on public health, were ignored; continuing with the war became a priority.

When these pressures, related to the war, are taken into consideration it is not surprising that the Provisional Government struggled to maintain authority. The government was unlucky in that it was formed late in the war when much of the damage to the economy and military had already occurred. In this respect, this view holds some weight. However, critics of this perspective have argued that the Provisional Government was doomed to failure regardless of the war.

Some argue that the Provisional Government stood little chance.

- The peoples of the Russian Empire viewed the Provisional Government as simply a variation on the tsarist regime. In fact, the Empire was in danger of disintegrating before the First World War; the new government struggled to contain demands for autonomy from Finland, Poland and Ukraine (all major agricultural areas).
- Workers had already organised and campaigned for economic and social change before the war. By 1917, the soviets were in such a strong position (see below) that the Provisional Government was compelled to join with them to create a dual authority. This is evidence that the groundswell of popular protest had gained momentum over at least a decade and it was only a matter of time before the proletariat took control of the governance of Russia.
- Kerensky's leadership was suspect, especially when it came to dealing with opposition from Kornilov (see page 60). He was not trusted by the workers and peasants even though he had a socialist background.

This view is convincing to an extent; it stresses the need to see the 1917 Revolutions as an event resulting from a multitude of pressures that built up over a long period of time and there is much evidence to support this. However, it downplays the impact of the First World War by suggesting that it affected Russia in a similar way to previous wars (that is by highlighting the essential weakness and corruption of imperial Russia). In that respect, it was not unique. This ignores the point that the war was the first global, total war and, by definition, would have had a much greater effect than any military conflict witnessed before.

The challenge from the Petrograd Soviet

From the outset authority was shared with the Petrograd Soviet (thus creating what is known as the Dual Authority), who opposed most of the Provisional Government's proposals. The Provisional Government had little option but to coalesce with the Soviet given the degree of popular support the latter had from workers, peasants, soldiers and sailors. The two groups disagreed, though, over Russia's involvement in the war. The Provisional Government wanted to push on for 'a decisive victory' while the Petrograd Soviet demanded 'peace without annexations or indemnities', and also 'revolutionary defencism'. The Provisional Government's stance

Alexander Kerensky 1881–1970

Kerensky first rose to prominence as a SR member of the *Duma* of 1912. He is best known for his role in the Provisional Government, initially as minister of justice, then as minister of war and finally as prime minister. He fled when other members of the Provisional Government were arrested by the Bolsheviks in October 1917. He later settled in the USA.

Peace without annexations or indemnities

This refers to a peace deal being reached without Russia having to hand over territory to its opponents (Germany and Austria-Hungary) and without having to pay any compensation.

Revolutionary defencism

The term refers to the defence and protection of everything achieved by the revolution of March 1917.

was understandable; some success had been achieved on the Eastern front in preventing a total German victory with the minimum of diversionary help from Russia's allies on the Western front. The war had also captured the imagination of the populace; although some called for peace this would have to be seen as honourable (that is, as the Soviet pointed out, 'without annexations or indemnities'). Thus, there is an argument that the Provisional Government had its hands tied over continuing the war, but this policy was likely to undermine its stability.

The issue of the eight principles

The first Provisional Government established a set of eight principles by which it would rule (see the box on the left). These were classically liberal and included decrees on political amnesty and full freedom of speech. However, this allowed for the proliferation of protest groups such as the Bolsheviks.

The lack of reforms

Despite the fact that the Provisional Government achieved its main aim of preparing a path for a constituent assembly, historians, such as Martin McCauley in *Russia 1917–1941* (1997), have claimed that it could have carried out economic and social reforms that would have helped it maintain power. This would then have given the temporary regime the chance to prepare more thoroughly for elections to the new assembly. McCauley claims that 'the greatest feature of the government was inactivity'. His view is that the Provisional Government did the following but this was not enough to appease workers and peasants:

- political prisoners were released
- secret courts were ended
- freedom of the press was introduced.

The major issues of worker demands for an eight-hour day and peasant demands for more land were largely ignored. Furthermore, the government's policy of continuation of the war resulted in food shortages, inflation and demonstrations by workers, soldiers and sailors. By not making more reforms, the Provisional Government is considered to have led to rejection by most of the army and population. Hence, by the time the Constituent Assembly was put in place there was much grassroots scepticism about whether it would succeed.

The counter-argument to this is that the early changes made by the Provisional Government were not intended as reforms, but as principles that would aid major political change. The lack of an economic and social programme of reform was understandable given the war situation. McCauley's claim that there was a lack of urgency about the government can be challenged given the scope of internal and external challenges it faced.

Opposition from the Bolsheviks

Changes made by the Provisional Government facilitated the revival of political groups such as the Bolsheviks, whose leaders had been in exile. Stalin moved back to Petrograd from exile in Siberia in March 1917, and Lenin from Switzerland in April. Lenin moved quickly to publish his April Theses in which he condemned the Provisional Government for being bourgeois (middle class), and called for a seizure of power by the Soviet. Bolshevik leaders used propaganda and slogans, especially the promise

> **Eight Principles**
>
> The eight principles set out by the Provisional Government.
> 1. An immediate general amnesty for all political and religious offences, including terrorist acts, military revolts, agrarian offenses, and so on.
> 2. Freedom of speech and press; freedom to form labour unions and to strike. These political liberties should be extended to the army in so far as war conditions permit.
> 3. The abolition of all social, religious and national restrictions.
> 4. Immediate preparation for the calling of a constituent assembly, elected by universal and secret vote, which shall determine the form of government and draw up the Constitution for the country.
> 5. In place of the police, to organise a national militia with elective officers, and subject to the local self-governing body.
> 6. Elections to be carried out on the basis of universal, direct, equal and secret suffrage.
> 7. The troops that have taken part in the revolutionary movement shall not be disarmed or removed from Petrograd.
> 8. On duty and in war service, strict military discipline should be maintained, but when off duty, soldiers should have the same public rights as are enjoyed by other citizens.

of 'Peace, Bread and Land', to appeal for support from both workers and peasants. The Provisional Government struggled to deal with the Bolsheviks directly. Although leading Bolsheviks were exiled or imprisoned after the disturbances of the July Days (see below), Kerensky aided a Bolshevik revival by involving the Red Guard in the resolution of the Kornilov affair (see page 60).

Continuation of the peasant land problem

The peasant land issue dragged on (see pages 15-17). Owing to the nature of the problem, the Provisional Government argued that only an elected assembly could deal with it. This irritated peasant groups who wanted more immediate action to be taken.

The perceived unequal distribution of good quality land had been a major cause of peasant unrest since they were emancipated in 1861. The February Revolution seemed to give peasants hope that the a major land redistribution would be enacted by the new government as started to take over landowners' estates. But the government failed to do this and peasants across Russia reacted by illegally seizing land from landlords, Disturbances in the countryside proved to be a daily occurrence throughout 1917 and the government appeared at a loss as to how to react. The majority of members of the government were landowners themselves; they never seemed interested in enacting reforms that would be detrimental to their own self-interests.

The failure of coalition government

An attempt to unite the Provisional Government and Petrograd Soviet was made in May 1917, when a coalition government was formed. This was led by Prince Lvov, who invited six members of the Petrograd Soviet to join. However, national elections to a constituent assembly were postponed, the land issue was ignored, workers' committees were suppressed and involvement in the war continued. All of this lessened support for the Provisional Government and caused rising militancy within the Petrograd Soviet.

Prince Georgy Lvov 1861–1925

Lvov was descended from Rus princes. A civil servant he sat in the *Dumas* and later took an important role in trying to coordinate wartime supplies in a joint committee of *Duma* members and businessmen and industrialists. He was a prominent landowner and progressive reformer and the ex-chairman of the Union of Zemstva. From March to July 1917 he headed the Provisional Government. He died in poverty in exile in Paris.

Joseph Stalin 1879–1953

Stalin was born as Iosif Vissarionovich Dzhugashvili in Georgia. By 1905, Stalin started to represent local branches of Bolshevik Party (Georgia and South Russia) at conferences and, in 1912, he was elected to the Central Committee of the Bolsheviks. He was exiled in 1913 but by 1917 he was back in Russia and started to form a friendship with Lenin. From 1917 to 1922, Stalin was a specialist on national minorities' issues and active as a commander during the **Civil War**. He was appointed General Secretary of the Communist Party in 1922 before becoming involved in a dispute with Trotsky, Kamenev and Zinoviev over who was to lead Russia after Lenin's death (see page 103). Through skilful manipulation of individuals and factions, Stalin was able to control the Party Congress and subsequently expelled his main rivals from the party itself. He was, by 1928, effectively the leader of Russia. Stalin is usually associated with a level of repression that was unprecedented in Russian history. He is also credited with industrialising Russia and ensuring that the Russian people were able to defeat Nazi Germany. However, there is much debate over the Stalinist era, with a number of historians claiming that Stalin's personal role in key developments has been exaggerated.

Pravda

Pravda, (meaning Truth), started publication in May 1912 and quickly became the main Bolshevik newspaper. It was temporarily shut down by Kerensky, only to remerge after October 1917 as the main voice of the Communist Party of the Soviet Union. It held this position until the fall of the Soviet Union in 1991.

Lev Kamenev 1883–1936

Lev Kamenev was a leading Bolshevik revolutionary and later in his life a prominent politician in the Soviet Union. He was one of the original group of Politburo members (formed in 1917), which also included Lenin, Trotsky and Stalin. In the last years of Lenin's life he served as acting premier. Stalin viewed him with suspicion and, after he became leader, had Kamenev executed.

Lavr Kornilov 1870–1918

Kornilov was appointed as the new commander-in-chief of the armed forces in July 1917. After the attempted coup he was arrested and imprisoned, but as soon as he was released he formed the anti-Bolshevik Volunteer Army. He died fighting in the early stages of the Civil War.

Red Guard

A force of some 10,000 individuals, largely made up at this time of recruits from among the workers in factories who acted as the militia of the Bolsheviks.

The significance of the July Days (3–6 July)

The July Days was a three-day period of social unrest or, according to Trotsky, 'semi-insurrection' characterised by:

- confusion over who started it (Bolsheviks or Mensheviks?)
- general disorder (rioting and violence against the authorities) in Petrograd
- disunity (some workers attacked fellow workers who thought the protests were premature)
- the use of troops to easily put down the protests.

The significance of the July Days was that it raised the profile of Kerensky who was given credit for effectively handling the unrest. Two days after the protests had been stopped Kerensky was appointed prime minister. He quickly proceeded to clamp down on the Bolsheviks, shutting down the newspaper *Pravda* and arresting Trotsky and Kamenev, while Lenin was forced once more into exile. Thus, it looked as though Kerensky was the right appointment and was on his way to achieving stability in Russia. However, within months the new Russian premier revealed his weaknesses: he failed to convince all members of the government of his view that Russia should continue in the war and to deal with the land distribution issue. He also created a new crisis by mishandling the Kornilov affair.

The Kornilov Affair

The historian Ian Thatcher has suggested that opposition in the form of Kornilov was the turning point in the fortunes of the Provisional Government. In August 1917, the military commander, Kornilov, marched with his troops towards Petrograd with the intention of forcibly closing down the Soviet. Kerensky seemed to believe that Kornilov, having defeated the Soviet, would then move on to take over the Provisional Government and impose a military-style dictatorship. Kerensky, therefore, agreed to the militia of the Bolsheviks (the Red Guard) being given arms to defend Petrograd. In the end, a bloody conflict was averted. Railway workers refused to transport Kornilov's army. Kornilov also received advance warning of how quickly the Bolsheviks had mobilised their defences and decided that the proposed takeover had a good chance of ending in disaster. He therefore abandoned his plan and was arrested.

Thatcher has argued that the Kornilov affair was significant for a number of reasons.

- The Bolsheviks were viewed as heroes for organising the protection of Petrograd. They (the Red Guard and members of the Petrograd Soviet) were also 'armed' by the Provisional Government: a recipe for disaster.
- It was evident that the Provisional Government was susceptible to being challenged by the military and therefore by others who might want to use force to seize power.
- Kerensky was shown to be a weak leader compared with Lenin (who was showing his mettle as a party leader, mostly from exile).
- After the affair, the Bolsheviks quickly gained more support because they were seen as heroes in defending the Revolution so that by early September they had majorities in both the Petrograd and Moscow Soviets. By the end of October, they had ousted the Provisional Government and taken control of Petrograd.

Overall, the Provisional Government struggled to deal with its opponents but this was probably more to do with circumstance than its incompetence.

Members of the Red Guard at the Vulkan Factory, Petrograd, in October 1917

The role of national minorities

Opposition towards the Provisional Government from national minorities is a factor that is sometimes overlooked when analysing the reasons for its demise. This is mainly because of the emphasis placed on the impact of the First World War and other problems inherited by the Provisional Government. One line of thought is that as the Provisional Government's main aim was to maintain the cohesiveness of the state until a constituent assembly could be established, it should have been a priority to assert authority across the whole of the empire. Instead, the Provisional Government focused mainly on urban political, economic and social issues especially in Petrograd and Moscow. Some historians have stressed this was a mistake.

- Minorities became frustrated that their wants and needs were not being addressed. The Provisional Government was blamed for being too slow to create an assembly, even though it was hard to see how the elections to the assembly could have been held earlier, given the circumstances of the war. An assembly would have then allowed minorities to express their views and would reduce resentment and calls for autonomy.
- Minorities were spurred on by the successes of workers, soldiers and sailors in establishing committees to demand more rights from employers and the government.
- Minorities took advantage of the 'principles' adopted by the Provisional Government on which administration of the state was to be based particularly the abolition of police units and provincial governors.

As a result, certain national minorities started to organise their own forms of provincial government, thus creating the possibility of the disintegration of the empire.

- A central *Rada* (council) was formed in Kiev in the Ukraine; its main aim was to press for the Ukraine to have autonomy.
- Similarly, in Finland, politicians campaigned for their own *Sejm* (parliament) free from the influence of central Russian government.

However, such moves were not ignored by the Provisional Government, as demands for self-rule in **Transcaucasia** were met with the formation of a Special Transcaucasian Committee. The problem with such initiatives though, as in other regions such as Estonia and Latvia, was that they were

Russia 1894–1941

> **Activity**
>
> The Provisional Government faced a number of challenges. Consider the following issues and find evidence of both success and failure in how well the Provisional Government dealt with each issue.
> - Legitimacy and relationship with the Soviet
> - War
> - The land question
> - Urban unrest
> - National minorities
> - Bolsheviks
> - Kornilov
> - Social and economic problems
>
> Having weighed up the evidence, do you think that the problems facing the Provisional Government made its downfall likely, or was it the actions that it took? Explain your answer.

> **The October/November revolution date issue**
>
> The events of the Bolshevik revolution which took place on 24 and 25 October by the Russian calendar were known in the USSR as the October Revolution. However, Russia used a different calendar from Western Europe until February 1918 when the Bolshevik regime lost 1 to 13 February and began on 14 February to use the Gregorian calendar of the West. By this calendar the revolution had taken place on 5 and 6 of November. The term October Revolution is the most usual way to refer to the Bolshevik takeover, but it actually happened in November 1917.

often undermined by the formation of local soviets. This illustrates how more general issues of autonomy for regions were tied up with the more particular concerns of workers and peasants. When bodies such as the *Rada* and *Sejm* stated they would deal with local social and economic problems such as land distribution they appeared to become a layer of unofficial opposition to policies emanating from Petrograd.

On the one hand, it seems reasonable to emphasise that the fortunes of the Provisional Government rested on how well they dealt with the challenges of a lack of legitimacy, the land question, urban unrest and the First World War. On the other hand, it is important to consider the strength of opposition from national minorities to the government and how the latter seemed to underestimate the strength of feeling at regional level. Given that, for example in Georgia, Estonia and the Ukraine, the majority of the population were peasants, it seems naive for the Provisional Government not to have prioritised dealing with the land transference issue. Not getting a grip on the rise of nationalism in the regions of the Empire undoubtedly caused the Provisional Government further problems as it enabled more left-wing parties at a local level to gain support.

Why was there a revolution in October 1917?

By the end of 1917, the Bolsheviks were responsible for the governance of Russia; a genuine revolution in Russian government had occurred. There were a number of key events that led to the final Bolshevik takeover in 1917.

First, on 8 September, the Bolsheviks gained control of the Petrograd Soviet. By the middle of September, they also controlled the Moscow Soviet. This prompted Lenin to return from Finland where he had once more been in exile. By 10 October, Lenin and his associates had started to formulate a plan for revolution.

Second, having become aware of increased Bolshevik activity, Kerensky responded by, on 23 October, closing *Pravda* and *Izvestiya* (another Bolshevik newspaper). A round-up of leading Bolsheviks was attempted but with mixed results. Trotsky was left to influence the setting up and running of the Petrograd Soviet's Military Revolutionary Committee (MRC). The MRC was partly a response by the Soviet to the possibility of another Kornilov-type attempted coup occurring, but also because it was feared German forces might soon be in a position to advance on the major Russian cities. Thus, the MRC was viewed primarily as a body to organise the defence of Petrograd from attack, but Trotsky realised the potential it might have in aiding the forceful overthrow of the government.

Third, just three days after the formation of the MRC, the members of the Provisional Government were arrested, except Kerensky, who fled. On the 27 October, the Second All-Russian Congress of Soviets (sitting since 25 October) was informed by Lenin that the Bolsheviks had taken power. The Congress was a meeting of soviet representatives who had been discussing how the soviets should deal with events as they had unfolded over the previous few months. By 2 November, the Bolsheviks also had control of Moscow and not long after the Congress of Soviets ratified Lenin's pronouncement of a Bolshevik takeover. The second revolution of 1917 was complete.

The October Revolution in the form of the overthrow of the Provisional Government and the short-lived Constituent Assembly was achieved with very little force and bloodshed. The series of events of the revolution are obviously quite complex. It is useful to untangle them further by considering how the Bolsheviks took control of Russia so easily.

Strength of opposition leadership: Lenin and Trotsky

In general, the Bolshevik leadership was more focused, determined and confident, supporting and harnessing the power of the Soviet, than any other interested group. This was especially true of Lenin and Trotsky.

Lenin

'Popular' support, as measured by numbers protesting on the streets and supporting the soviets, for radical change gathered momentum after September. Despite reservations from other senior Bolsheviks, Lenin, from exile, stressed the need to take advantage of this. In particular, Lenin's importance in determining what happened can be seen through the following.

- Lenin played on the weaknesses of the Provisional Government and Kerensky who had not solved the war and land issues.
- Lenin used his intellect and oratory skills to offer a gloomy prediction of what would happen if the Bolsheviks did not take advantage of circumstance (on the 12 September he wrote that 'History will not forgive us if we do not assume power').
- Lenin also continued to use slogans (especially 'All Power to the Soviets') to stress the importance of continued collaboration with workers.
- Lenin was very astute in pointing out that as October drew closer a number of developments would greatly hinder the Bolshevik chances of success: that is, the October meeting of the All-Russian Congress of Soviets; the election of the Constituent Assembly.

Overall, these qualities showed that Lenin was a far more capable strategist and tactician than leaders of other parties and of the Provisional Government.

The Bolshevik Revolution in Petrograd

On 24 October Kerensky ordered the closure of the Bolshevik newspaper but the MRC regained control of it. There were clashes over control of the bridges which Kerensky ordered to be raised to cut off the workers district from the main city. The MRC occupied the telegraph office.

On 25 October a take over of key points in the city was undertaken on orders from the MRC, organised by Trotsky, with Red Guards seizing communications such as railway stations. There was no resistance as the soldiers of the garrison and sailors and marines from the Kronstadt naval base joined the take over. The government head quarters at the Winter Palace was abandoned by its defenders and then occupied without bloodshed first by a few revolutionaries then, in the early hours of 26 October by a mass of workers and soldiers. The ministers were arrested but Kerensky had fled.

Key events in the Bolshevik seizure of power September–October 1917

September 25	The Bolsheviks gained a majority in the Petrograd Soviet
October 9	Petrograd Soviet established the Military Revolutionary Committee (MRC)
October 11	Zinoviev and Kamenev opposed Lenin's idea of an uprising
October 23	Kerensky ordered the closing down of Bolshevik papers. Lenin ordered the rising to start
October 24	Congress of Soviets starts
October 24–5	Bolsheviks took control of Petrograd (see text box on page 63)
October 25–6	Kerensky fled from Petrograd. Bolsheviks seized the Winter Palace
October 26	Bolsheviks established Sovnarkom
October 27	Lenin claimed power in the name of the Congress of Soviets

Trotsky

Trotsky's role can be traced back to 1905, when he was first appointed as chairman of the St Petersburg Soviet. After that, his influence can be seen through the following:

- his period in exile (1907–17), when he developed his ideas about Permanent Revolution
- his return in September 1917 as chairman of the Petrograd Soviet; on 9 October, the Soviet set up the MRC to organise the defence of Petrograd (against a possible German attack)
- Trotsky officially became one of three co-ordinators of the MRC realising that he might be able to influence it (the only legitimate, organised military unit in the capital) to challenge the Provisional Government
- his management of the Red Guards (initially, a force of about 10,000 male workers recruited from factories); although not new, the Red Guards became the militia of the MRC and Bolshevik Party
- from 25 to 27 October it was the Red Guards who ousted the Provisional Government suffering just six casualties.

Thus, Trotsky played a crucial role in organising and administering the forces required for the Bolsheviks to take control of the governance of Russia. However, his achievements need to be qualified. Trotsky was a member of the MRC, but he did not dominate it. The MRC consisted mainly of worker representatives drawn from a variety of backgrounds who showed allegiance to a number of different political parties (not just the Bolsheviks). Additionally, the Provisional Government proved to be totally unprepared and hapless in dealing with the MRC; the Petrograd garrison, in particular, was sadly depleted as a result of desertions. By October, it consisted of a few Cossacks, some officer cadets and a group female soliders known as **Amazons**. Thus, the government had very little to fall back on (compared with the July Days), in the way of armed forces.

Weaknesses of the Provisional Government

As Lenin emphasised, the Provisional Government had failed to deliver when it came to the war and the land issue. However, Kerensky attempted to counter this by stating that a 'pre-parliament' would be established, with members being taken from the existing political parties. The 'pre-parliament' would advise the government on what was to be done before a constituent assembly could be elected. Kerensky believed this would send out a clear message to the masses that their views were going to be listened to and that the new Assembly would focus on dealing with issues that were most pressing. Lenin dismissed this as Kerensky's attempt to save his own neck; subsequently the Bolsheviks steered well away from the idea of a 'pre-parliament.'

Lenin returned to Petrograd from exile in Finland on 7 October and urged, even more strongly, for the Bolsheviks to take over. Kerensky attempted to deal with this by once again, on 23 October, rounding up leading Bolsheviks and shutting down *Pravda* and *Izvestiya*. However, this proved to be too late; Lenin was in a strong position by this time (although he regarded the situation as desperate). Lenin believed the Bolsheviks had to act before it was too late and, with some trepidation ordered the start of the planned overthrow.

Leon Trotsky 1879–1940

Trotsky started his political career as a Menshevik. In 1905, he was appointed chairman of the St Petersburg Soviet but was exiled until 1917. When Trotsky returned to Russia he joined the Bolshevik party and was appointed chairman of the Petrograd Soviet. He then became the organiser of the October Revolution. On 9 October, as chairman, he influenced the Petrograd Soviet to set up the MRC. This meant that the Soviet had the means to control Petrograd. Trotsky built on this by organising the Red Guard, which took control of the strategic locations of administration in Petrograd. After the Revolution, Trotsky was given the role as the main negotiator of the Treaty of Brest-Litovsk. He then went on to establish and manage the Red Army during the Civil War (1918–21) to great effect. After Lenin's death, Trotsky became embroiled in a power struggle for the leadership, which he lost, and then, as a result of antagonising Stalin, he was assassinated (while in exile in Mexico in 1940) under a directive from the Russian leader.

Weaknesses of parties other than the Bolsheviks

There were three evident trends, with respect to the non-Bolshevik parties and groups that would explain why they were not interested in toppling the existing order.

- Liberals (the Kadets in particular) and SR were relatively satisfied that a revolution had already occurred (in March 1917) and wanted to wait until the Constituent Assembly was working. As the Provisional Government was dominated by liberals, Lenin was able to suggest that the SR had colluded with bourgeois elements and had betrayed the revolution.
- The other parties largely supported the Provisional Government's decision to keep Russia at war (albeit for different reasons). Lenin was determined to show that this was a mistake and detrimental to the long-term future of Russia.
- The Mensheviks continued to oppose the Bolsheviks for both practical and ideological reasons; they believed the **proletariat** were not strong and able enough to take control of Russia. They pushed for consolidation of the gains of March 1917 (the end of tsarism) arguing that this corresponded with the Marxist view that the last vestiges of feudalism had been vanquished thus paving the way for a genuine workers' revolution. This view resulted in collaboration with other parties and groups but in turn they were blinkered to the opportunities created by the failings of Kerensky's government.

Popular support

The revolution of 1917 undoubtedly happened as a result of pressure from below. This was especially evident through the proliferation of soviets, the rapid setting up of the MRC and rising affiliation to the Bolshevik Party. Without popular support the Bolshevik Party would have floundered. The Mensheviks underestimated the determination and abilities of the soviets to challenge the Provisional Government. However, the exact level of popular support is difficult to calculate and this has caused some commentators to down play this factor. Also, the Bolsheviks came to dominate the soviets before the October coup; in this respect, the revolution was a triumph for Lenin and Trotsky, masking the contribution played by earlier soviet leaders.

What were the consequences of the revolution?

The impact of the revolution at first glance seems obvious. The Bolshevik seizure of power was truly revolutionary in that it put an end to government by a regime associated, via the *Duma*, with Russia's autocratic past. The promise, at the time, was that the Provisional Government would be replaced initially by the dictatorship of the proletariat, which would eventually give way to a stateless society, that is, communism. If this had succeeded, then the consequences of the revolution would have been truly momentous, not just for Russia but probably for the rest of the world. However, for a variety of reasons, the dictatorship *of* the proletariat was transformed into a situation whereby Lenin dictated *to* the proletariat, and the rest of Russian society.

Dictatorship under Stalin, akin to that which emerged in other parts of Europe during the inter-war period (especially with Hitler and Mussolini) became a form of totalitarianism. It could be argued that this was an extreme form of autocracy. It is no wonder that this has led to claims that the tsars were simply replaced with red tsars; leaders who were different in appearance and background but almost identical in terms of how they ruled. This would mean that the revolution, in conjunction with the First World War and the Civil War, did not really result in major changes to the governance of Russia even though the events themselves appeared dramatic.

Activity

The focus in this section has been on why the Bolsheviks were able to overthrow the Provisional Government. Examination questions are often set that ask you to 'Assess the reasons why the Bolsheviks were successful in October 1917'. However, in considering this issue, it is important that you assess the factors and do not simply produce a list.

1 In order to address this question, you should identify five possible reasons, explain how they led to Bolshevik success, but most importantly analyse their importance. This might be done through a table similar to the one below.

Factor leading to Bolshevik success	Explanation of the factor	Mark out of six for importance: 0 = little importance; 6 = very important	Explanation of judgement

2 Which was the most important factor? Explain your answer.

3 It might also be helpful to think of links between the factors. Are there any factors that link together? Explain the links.

Historical debate

Why did the tsar abdicate in February 1917?

The events of 1917 have provoked considerable debate among historians, both over the importance of the First World War in the collapse of the tsarist regime, but also the nature of the Bolshevik takeover in October 1917. The two passages below consider the issue of the collapse of the tsarist regime.

Passage 1

After 1914 an unbridgeable chasm was opening up between the government and the people. In fact, who or what was the government? It changed so quickly, no-one could be quite sure. In the first two years of war four prime ministers came and went. The railway system in the western provinces and Poland proved inadequate. Through the closing of the Baltic and Black Sea ports, Russia was cut off from her allies. The low level of technical and economic development produced an army suffering a paralysing shortage of equipment and trained personnel. Many soldiers often had no weapons at all: they were expected to arm themselves from the discarded rifles of the killed and wounded. Shells had to be rationed to the artillery batteries. Hospital and medical services were so thinly spread that they had no practical value. The call-up operated irrationally, amounting in 1917 to some 15 million – around 37 per cent of the males of working age. Chaos piled upon chaos with the influx of refugees. Inflation, food shortages and a fall in real wages produced an increasing ordeal for the mass of the population. A mounting wave of strikes gave voice and vent not only to economic demands. 'Down with the Tsar' was the ominous cry beginning to be heard. In a word, the war had utterly destroyed any confidence that still remained between the government and the people.

Lionel Kochan, *The Making of Modern Russia*, 1962

Passage 2

Russia without a Tsar in the people's minds was a contradiction in terms; for them it was the person of the Tsar that defined and gave reality to the state. In view of this tradition, one might have expected the mass of the population to favour the retention of the monarchy. But two factors militated against such a stand. The peasantry remained monarchistic. Nevertheless, in early 1917 it was not averse to an interlude of anarchy, sensing it would provide the opportunity finally to carry out a nationwide 'Black Partition' (wholesale redistribution of land). The other consideration had to do with the fear of punishment on the part of the Petrograd populace, especially the troops. The February events could be seen in different ways, as a glorious revolution or as a sordid mutiny. If the monarchy survived it was likely to view the actions as mutiny. When he arrived at Pskov on 1 March 1917 Nicholas had no thoughts of abdicating. In his diary of the previous day he noted he had sent a message to General Ivanov in Petrograd to 'introduce order'. In the twenty-four hours that followed, Nicholas heard from everyone that as long as he remained Tsar, Russia could not win the war. He paid heed to the generals. Telegram after telegram from the military commanders urged him, for the sake of the country, first to allow the Duma to form a cabinet and then to abdicate. All the evidence is that Nicholas abdicated from patriotic motives to spare Russia a humiliating defeat. If his foremost concern had been to preserve his throne, he could easily have made peace with Germany and used front-line troops to crush the rebellion in Petrograd and Moscow. He chose instead to give up his crown and save the front.

Richard Pipes, *The Russian Revolution 1899–1919*, 1990

Activity

1. In light of the two passages and further research, do you agree that it was the weakness of the tsar that was the main reason for the revolution in March 1917?
2. Using the information in this and the previous chapter, find evidence to support the two views.
   - It was the war that caused the Revolution in March 1917.
   - It was long-term structural problems in the tsar's regime that caused the Revolution in March 1917.
3. Which of the two views do you find more convincing? Explain your choice.
4. Is there any way the two views can be combined to give a more convincing explanation of the March 1917 Revolution.

Further Research

Neil Faulkner, *A People's History of the Russian Revolution*, Pluto Press, 1917

Sheila Fitzpatrick, *The Russian Revolution 1917–1932*, Oxford University Press, 1994

Stephen Kotkin, *Stalin Paradoxes of Power 1878–1928*, Allen Lane, 2014

Dominic Lieven, *Towards the Flame: Empire, War and the End of Tsarist Russia*, Allen Lane, 2015

Richard Pipes, *The Russian Revolution 1899–1919*, CollinsHarvill, 1990

Christopher Read, *Lenin*, Routledge, 2005

Richard Sakwa, *The Rise and Fall of the Soviet Union 1917–1991*, Routledge, 1999

Victor Sebestyen, *Lenin an Intimate Portrait*, Weidenfeld & Nicolson, 2017

Ian D. Thatcher (ed.), *Regime and Society in Twentieth-Century Russia*, Macmillan, 1999

Leon Trotsky, *History of the Russian Revolution*, Penguin, 2017

Chapter takeaways

- The First World War had a dramatic impact on the political, economic and social life of Russia. A poor military showing led to a lowering of morale and disenchantment with the leadership of Nicholas II.
- The leadership of the tsar during the war period left much to be desired. He seemed to lack effective judgement over military strategy, tactics and appointments. By taking control of the armed forces in 1915 he made an enormous gamble that failed to pay off.
- An added problem for the governance during the First World War was the influence of the mystic monk, Rasputin, over the tsarina. However, the negative impact of his presence and role in general has probably been exaggerated.
- Nicholas was pushed by the fourth *Duma* to be decisive and proactive as a wartime leader. The *Duma* was instrumental in persuading the tsar to abdicate.
- The abdication of Nicholas II in March 1917 constituted a revolution. It ended over 300 years of Romanov rule and led to the setting up of a Provisional Government. The Provisional Government attempted a liberal rather than autocratic approach to governing but struggled to deal with the challenges it faced.
- The Provisional Government struggled to survive partly due to its lack of credibility but also as a result of the great magnitude of the problems it inherited. It was forced into an alliance with the Petrograd Soviet and never really got to grips with having to share power.
- The October Revolution was a result of building pressures for change over months maybe even years. The Bolsheviks, in conjunction with support from the soviets (the Petrograd Soviet in particular), were able to take advantage of deteriorating economic, social and political conditions to wrest authority from the Provisional Government and to impose their own style of rule.

Study skills: Writing an introduction and avoiding irrelevance

The types of question set for AS and A Level essays will be the same and therefore all the advice in this section applies to both examinations.

Writing an introduction

Having planned your answer to the question, as described in the previous chapter, you are in a position to write your crucial opening paragraph. This should set out your main line of argument and briefly refer to the issues you are going to cover in the main body of the essay. The essays will require you to reach a judgement about the issue in the question. It is a good idea to state in this vital opening paragraph what overall judgement you are going to make.

It might also be helpful, in the opening paragraph, to define key terms mentioned in the question.

Consider the question in the example box:

> **Example**
>
> **Assess the reasons why Nicholas II abdicated in March 1917.**
>
> In the opening paragraph of an answer to this question you should:
>
> - Identify the issues or themes that you will consider – these might be the failures of Russia's war efforts, social unrest in Petrograd, opposition from the Progressive Bloc in the *Duma*
> - State your view as to which of the factors was the most important.

This type of approach will help you to keep focused on the demands of the question ('reasons why') rather than writing a general essay about the tsar's abdication. It might also be helpful to occasionally refer back to the opening paragraph.

This approach will also ensure you avoid writing about the background to the topic, for example explaining the course of the First World War, which has little relevance to the actual question set. Another mistake is to fail to write a first paragraph that does not concur with the main body of the answer and the conclusion. Readers appreciate knowing the direction the essay is going to take, rather than embarking on a mystery tour where the line of argument becomes apparent only at the end.

The following is a sample of a good introductory paragraph:

> **Sample answer**
>
> Nicholas II abdicated in March 1917 under pressure from senior military advisers, members of the Progressive Bloc in the *Duma* and his family. The reasons why these individuals and groups pushed the tsar to step down relate primarily to how badly Russia had performed in the First World War and how the war had led to considerable hardship for the Russian people.
>
> The latter was increasingly associated with unrest in Petrograd by early 1917 and it was this that provoked the pressure for abdication to intensify. Above all, Nicholas must take the blame for his own abdication as he failed to offer effective leadership during the war and often appeared indifferent to how it was progressing.

The paragraph offers a view as to the most important reason for the abdication, but also outlines some of the other factors that the essay will consider. It remains focused on the question throughout the paragraph and shows some understanding of the key developments and events that occurred during this period. The answer shows a sound knowledge of why the abdication occurred and is able to use that knowledge to put forward a clear argument.

Avoiding irrelevance

You should take care not to write irrelevant material as this will not gain marks; it also wastes your time. Take the following precautions to avoid this.

- Look carefully at the wording of the question.
- Avoid simply writing all you know about the topic; remember you need to select information relevant to the actual question. Use such information to support an argument and to reach an overall judgement about the issue in the question.

- Revise *all* of a topic so that you are not tempted to pad out a response with waffle as a result of not having enough material directly relevant to the actual question.

Consider the following question:

> ### Example
>
> **How influential was the Petrograd Soviet on the work of the Provisional Government from March to October 1917?**
>
> You should:
>
> - consider the aims and objectives of the Petrograd Soviet and their actions towards the Provisional Government so that you can establish criteria against which to judge their influence
> - explain how far the actions impinged on the work of the Provisional Government
> - differentiate between actions that were influential and those that were not
> - consider the role of both bodies in the wider context of the challenges offered by Russia's continuation in the First World War
> - assess the level of impact of actions of the Petrograd Soviet on the work of the Provisional Government across the whole period.

The following is a sample of an irrelevant answer to the question above:

> ### Sample answer
>
> The influence of the Petrograd Soviet on the Provisional Government was significant. This is partially illustrated by the continuous disagreement between the Petrograd Soviet and the Provisional Government over Russia's involvement in the war. The former wanted to push on for 'a decisive victory' while the latter demanded 'peace without annexations or indemnities' (but also 'revolutionary defensism'). Protests against the war heightened and reached a disturbing peak in July when the sailors at Kronstadt mutinied. The rift was never resolved and was a major reason for the eventual failure of the government. An attempt to bridge the differences between the two competing authorities was made in May 1917 with the formation of a coalition government. This was led by Prince Lvov who invited six members of the Petrograd Soviet to join. Prince Lvov was from one of the most respected noble families. But it did little to appease the more radical members of the Soviet and the problems faced by the ruling body continued. National elections to a constituent assembly were postponed, the land issue was ignored, workers committees were clamped down on and involvement in the war continued. All of this combined to produce a further decline in support for the Provisional Government and rising militancy within the Petrograd Soviet.

The answer starts with some focus on the question but then proceeds to drift towards a narrative about the impact of the First World War and how the Petrograd Soviet and Provisional Government reacted to this. Relations between the two bodies are described rather than analysed and evaluated.

The comments are on the topic but not the exact demands of the question. Thus, the response shows little understanding of the question and is largely irrelevant. It is important to have a clear grasp of the basic concepts and the requirements of the question otherwise an answer soon loses focus.

Question practice

The focus of this section has been on avoiding irrelevance and writing a focused vital opening paragraph. Using the information from the chapter, write an opening paragraph to one of the essays below, ensuring that you keep fully focused on the question. It might also be helpful to consolidate the skill developed in the previous chapter by planning the answer before you start writing the paragraph.

1 'Economic dislocation was the most serious consequence of the First World War for Russian people.' How far do you agree?
2 To what extent was Rasputin responsible for Nicholas II's downfall?
3 To what extent was there a revolution in March 1917?
4 Assess the reasons for the limited success of the Provisional Government?
5 'There would have been no revolution in October 1917 without Lenin and Trotsky.' How far do you agree?

Short answer essay question

Which of the following had the greatest impact on the Provisional Government's attempt to rule Russia?
(i) The First World War
(ii) The land issue

Explain your answer with reference to both (i) and (ii).

The Civil War and Lenin

This chapter concerns the transition from revolution to civil war in Russia. It begins with an analysis of the short-lived Constituent Assembly before moving on to consider how Lenin started to consolidate power. The focus is then placed on the causes, course and consequences of the Russian Civil War and how this was linked to the establishment of communism. The consequences of the war were inextricably tied up with the early economic and political changes that were made by the Bolsheviks in their attempt to establish stability; these are assessed towards the end of the chapter with some final comments concerning Lenin's achievements as leader of Russia.

The chapter addresses a number of key questions.

- How significant was the formation of the Constituent Assembly?
- How did Lenin begin to consolidate Bolshevik power?
- What were the causes and course of the Russian Civil War (1918–21)?
- Why did the Bolsheviks win the Civil War (1918-21)?
- How significant was the New Economic Policy (NEP)?
- How successful was the creation of the new communist government and the constitutions?
- To what extent was Lenin a strong leader of the Bolsheviks?

This chapter will also focus on the skills of writing analytically and developing the crucial opening sentence of each paragraph in an essay. It will also explain what is meant by a descriptive answer and how to avoid writing these types of answers, which will score low marks. The chapter will stress the importance of the opening sentence of each paragraph and also of introducing an idea, which is linked to the question and will be discussed throughout the paragraph before making a judgement about the issue. These skills will help to ensure that the actual demands of the question are addressed and help you avoid simply writing all you know about the topic.

Timeline

1917	October	Decree on Peace
	November	Decrees on Land and Workers' Control
1918	Summer	Start of Russian Civil War (including foreign involvement)
	June	War Communism
1918	January	The dissolution of the Constituent Assembly; Formation of the Red Army
	March	Treaty of Brest-Litovsk
	June	Decree on Nationalisation
	July	Grain requisitioning (and start of famine)
		Tsar and his family murdered
	September	Red Terror
1919	March	Comintern set up
		Bolshevik Party changed name to Communist Party
1920	April	Polish armed forces pushed back Red Army
1921	March	Kronstadt rising
	April	Introduction of the New Economic Policy (NEP)
1924	January	Lenin's death

Overview

Once the Provisional Government was deposed, the Bolsheviks faced the prospect of the formation of a constituent assembly; Lenin and his associates were fairly confident they would gain a majority in the new elected body, but that proved not to be the case. Lenin reacted to the formation of the Assembly by challenging its legitimacy before shutting it down. Although this provoked outrage from the other political parties, especially the SR, Lenin insisted though that only the Bolsheviks were fit to rule and that this was the will of the peasants and workers.

Lenin faced two immediate problems after he and the Bolsheviks closed down the Constituent Assembly. First, he needed to tackle Russia's involvement in the First World War. Second, he had to confront and clamp down on opposition. After he dealt with these issues he then had to move on to further consolidate his position and win acceptance of the new Bolshevik regime from the rest of the world.

Lenin solved the war problem by authorising the signing of the Treaty of Brest-Litovsk in March 1918. This was a peace treaty with Germany and the terms for Russia were harsh.

Bolshevik authority was quickly established through the setting up of the Soviet of People's Commissars or *Sovnarkom*. This cabinet of leading Bolsheviks issued a number of decrees. These focused on banning opposition and were to be enforced through the use of a new secret police force, the **Cheka**. But opposition either went underground or was difficult to control because of the geographical size of Russia.

The strength and spread of opposition resulted in a **civil war**, which the Bolsheviks won by using the Red Army, the *Cheka* (secret police) and the policy of War Communism. War Communism and the tight control over economic life had become unpopular and opposition had arisen by 1923, which threatened Communist rule. In order to stabilise Russia, Lenin announced his New Economic Policy (NEP). The NEP was the main plank in Lenin's strategy to stabilise Russia and stimulate a rise in grain production. Lenin's death, in 1924, led to a power struggle. One of the issues debated was the viability and efficacy of the NEP. The 'right' communists wanted it to continue whereas the 'left' communists wanted it to be replaced. When Stalin emerged victorious from the struggle he quickly imposed a personalised style of rule and a raft of economic and social policies that mirrored his brand of communism.

How significant was the formation of the Constituent Assembly?

The Constituent Assembly was an elected body of representatives of the different groups that existed across the Russian Empire. Its main aim was to create a constitution under which Russia would be governed. After the abdication of Nicholas II, it was logical that laying the foundation for a constituent assembly would be the prime objective of the Provisional Government. The Provisional Government achieved what it set out to do but, when it was disbanded by the **Bolsheviks**, there was little indication that the Assembly would also be shut down within a short space of time.

Work in preparation for the elections to the Assembly had involved the input of the major political parties and organisations, including trade unions and soviets. Explanation of who was eligible to vote and how the elections would be conducted was done through the issuing of leaflets, posters and public lectures. Those parties who were to offer candidates for election also organised individual election campaigns.

In August 1917, the Provisional Government completed a draft of the Statute of Elections to the All-Russian Constituent Assembly. The Statute allowed for:
- the right to vote for all citizens (men and women) of the age of 20 and above
- the right to vote for all servicemen of the age of 18 and above.

These were radical provisions for the time: only Norway, Denmark, Finland, New Zealand, Australia and some American states had given the vote to women. The main features of the system of voting were as follows.

- Proportional representation: one deputy per 200,000 citizens was to be elected from within electoral districts (constituencies); some districts would have more deputies than others as a result of having larger populations. Siberia was an exception to this, being allocated one deputy per 179,000 people.
- The spreading of election times and dates (theoretically, from 12 to 14 November 1917; in practice, some occurred as late as January 1918).

There has been some debate over the accuracy of the figures for the election results. The general consensus among historians is that 67 electoral districts were involved with the casting of over 41 million votes.

Although the Bolsheviks had started to claim de facto rule, they failed to win a majority in elections to the Constituent Assembly. The results suggested that the degree of 'opposition' to them was substantial (see Table 1).

What were the results of the election?

Table 1 Results of the election to the Constituent Assembly

Party	Votes	Seats
SR	17,490,000	370
Bolsheviks	9,844,000	175
National minority groups	8,257,000	99
Left SR (pro-Bolshevik)	2,861,000	40
Kadets	1,986,000	17
Mensheviks	1,248,000	16
Total	41,686,000	

Source: M. Lynch, *Reaction and Revolution: Russia 1881–1924*, 2nd edition, Hodder Education, 2004, page 134.

The first (and last) meeting of the Constituent Assembly was held on 5 January 1918 at the Tauride Palace in Petrograd. The gathered deputies had time to elect a chairman (V.M. Chernov, the leader of the SR) before being challenged by Lenin as being unlawful and unrepresentative. Under Bolshevik threats at gun point the Assembly disbanded on 6 January 1918.

Why did the Bolsheviks disband the Constituent Assembly?

Lenin believed that the Bolsheviks would not be able to achieve and consolidate power through future elections to the Assembly, and therefore chose to use physical force to end it. More specifically, the official justification for such action was that:
- the will of the Russian people had already been expressed in the backing for the Bolshevik government that emerged from the October Revolution
- the elections to the Constituent Assembly had been rigged by the SR and Kadets, and that, 'The Russian soviets place the interests of the toiling masses far above the interests of treacherous compromise disguised in a new garb' (V. I. Lenin, 'Speech On The Dissolution Of The Constituent Assembly', 6 January 1918). Power handed to the Constituent Assembly would represent a 'compromise with the malignant bourgeoisie. Nothing in the world will induce us to surrender Soviet power.'

These justifications were hard to accept for some of Lenin's supporters, let alone those who opposed him.

What was the reaction?

Concerns were expressed within the Bolshevik party over the methods adopted by Lenin. For example, the well-known writer Maxim Gorky, who was close to the Bolsheviks, claimed Lenin was a 'cold blooded trickster who spares neither the honour nor life of the **proletariat**'. There was dismay over what some saw as the end of any chance of democracy in Russia.

Opposition from the other parties was, of course, substantial. The liberals and SR were outraged that the Assembly had been shut down but, given the amount of influence the Bolsheviks had gained at grassroots level, especially via the soviets, there was little they could do. Besides, the Bolsheviks had also organised the Red Guard to use force to impose their authority; the liberals and SR were not in a position to defend themselves against that kind of militia. Nevertheless, the SR in particular continued to voice their opposition and their abhorrence of Lenin was further strengthened by his desire to take Russia out of the First World War and strike a peace deal with Germany. However, it is worth noting that despite his issuing of the Theses on the Question of the Immediate Conclusion of a Separate and Annexationist Peace (20 January 1918), Lenin had private worries that if peace were made 'the capitalists of the whole word' would unite against revolutionary Russia. The 'left' SR, especially, saw Lenin as a traitor to the revolution and a German collaborator.

Despite opposition from political groups such as the SR, who claimed to have the interests of the people closer to their hearts than the Bolsheviks, there was little adverse reaction to the closure of the Assembly from peasants and workers. The peasantry had traditionally supported the SR but in this instance seemed intent on going about their day-to-day business, relying on village soviets as the main vehicle for expressing their grievances. One SR activist claimed he heard a peasant soldier state that 'What do we need some Constituent Assembly for when we have our Soviets, where our own deputies can meet and decide on everything.' If typical, this view did not suggest that the peasantry were ready to challenge Bolshevik authority.

> **Maxim Gorky 1868–1936**
>
> Maxim Gorky was a political activist and Russian writer, often credited with founding the literary method of socialist realism. On five occasions he was nominated for the Nobel Prize in Literature. His writing was informed by his experience of travelling across the Russian Empire at an early age. He was inspired, in particular, to record the lives of ordinary Russians and had strong feelings about the inequality and injustice he witnessed. Gorky was a staunch opponent of tsarism and sided with Lenin and the Bolsheviks. His political associations often got him in trouble and he was exiled on two occasions (1906–13 and 1921–32). He returned to Russia in 1932 at the invitation of Stalin but died from ill-health four years later.

Activity

1 Consider the following reasons as to why Lenin dissolved the Constituent Assembly.
   - Lenin had no faith in democratic elections.
   - Lenin was determined to prevent elections from undermining Bolshevik power.
   - Lenin believed in crushing opposition, not working with it.
   - The Bolshevik position was weak and he could not consider power sharing.
   - There was no need for the Assembly as the people had expressed their will in the October Revolution.
2 Which of these explanations do you think best explains the reasons for Lenin dissolving the Constituent assembly? Explain your answer.

How did Lenin begin to consolidate Bolshevik power?

The consolidation of Bolshevik power started after Lenin had gained control of Petrograd (25 October 1917) and had announced to the first session of the Second All-Russian Congress of Soviets that he had taken power. The **Mensheviks** and SR denounced the Bolshevik actions as a 'criminal venture';

they had hoped that the Congress would lead to the formation of a socialist government based on all the parties in the Congress of Soviets. In protest, they walked out of the Congress causing Trotsky to shout out, 'Go where you belong – to the rubbish bin of history!'; this was a mistake as it gave the Bolsheviks the chance to manipulate the rest of the delegates to condemn the behaviour of the Mensheviks and SR and to sanction the move towards a Bolshevik dominated government.

On 26 October, Lenin set up the Council of Peoples Commissars (*Sovnarkom*); this was designed to operate as the main government organ of the Bolsheviks and was to be directed by the Congress of Soviets. Its first step was to shut down the opposition press and order the arrest, using the MRC, of Menshevik, SR and Kadet leaders. This was followed shortly after by the announcement that Sovnarkom would pass legislation without the approval of the Congress of Soviets thus reneging on the initial principle on which it was established.

Clearly, steps towards a single-party dictatorship had been taken leaving a number of Bolsheviks nervous about the implications of this. Given that, despite the political turmoil, it was agreed that elections to the Constituent Assembly should go ahead, a number of Lenin's supporters thought their tenure in office would be short-lived. Lenin was aware of this and quickly took supplementary measures, in the form of decrees, to emphasise the strength of his government.

Council of Peoples Commissars (*Sovnarkom*)

The 'people's commissars' were ministers with specific governmental responsibilities (the word 'minister' was replaced by 'commissar' as the former was said to have bourgeois connotations). Trotsky, for example, was placed in charge of foreign affairs. The chairman (prime minister) was Lenin. To begin with the Council also consisted of left-wing SR. It was designed to act like a kind of parliamentary cabinet.

This new government body appeared to be democratic insofar as members of *Sovnarkom* were the product of a chain of elections:
- village soviets chose representatives for district soviets
- district soviets then elected members for the provincial soviets
- provincial soviets provided the membership of *Sovnarkom*.

However, the soviets were dominated by Bolshevik Party members; the organisation of the party was very similar to that of the new government.
- At local level, the party consisted of cells whose members would organise meetings (political workshops) to encourage grassroots support.
- Cell members were elected to town or district committees.
- Committees then provided representatives to the annual party congress.
- The Congress of Soviets chose members to form the party Central Executive Committee (consisting of about a tenth of congress members). In turn, the Central Executive Committee was responsible for the administration and operation of three political offices:
  1 The Politburo: a small, élite group of Bolsheviks responsible for formulating policy. The Politburo dominated the Central Committee and the running of the party.
  2 The Orgburo: this office organised party affairs.
  3 The Ogburo: this body was responsible for maintaining order and dealing with opposition.

Thus, the *Sovnarkom* was far from being a democratic institution and was designed more to be the machine for a dictatorial regime.

How were decrees used to consolidate power?

After deciding on the organisation of his government Lenin faced his most challenging problem; Russia's war situation. Through the Second Congress of Soviets the following announcement was made:

October 1917: The Decree on Peace. This asked for 'all belligerents to open negotiations without delay for a just and democratic peace ... a peace without annexations and indemnities.'

After much debate within the party and between parties, a peace agreement was reached, in March 1918, in the form of the Treaty of Brest-Litovsk. Russia struck a peace deal with Germany but only after agreeing to hand over valuable territory. For Lenin, this was an essential move as it shortened a conflict (the First World War) that was likely to end in total ruination of the economy. He also knew that it was likely to hasten the move towards civil war and the creation of further economic problems. Whatever, decision he took meant that the economy would in some way be adversely affected.

Treaty of Brest-Litovsk

The price of peace for Russia was high. Germany insisted on harsh territorial demands, labelled as 'massively punitive [punishing]' by the historian Steve Smith.

Much land was ceded to Germany that contained valuable resources. Russia lost: Poland, Estonia, Latvia, Lithuania, Ukraine, Georgia and Finland. All of these territories gained a form of independence, initially as German protectorates. This amounted to Russia losing one-third of its population (about 55 million people) as well as one-third of agricultural land, two-thirds of coalmines, one-half of heavy industry (iron and steel), nearly all available oil and most of cotton textile production.

Lenin knew these conditions were harsh. However, he believed the war would soon be over, that Germany would be defeated and that territory would be recovered. A greater hope was that a communist revolution would occur in Germany. The agreement also gave the Bolsheviks time to establish a government and to attend to other matters such as the state of the economy.

To help reassure the Russian peoples about how they might be treated under the new Russian government, Lenin and Stalin made an announcement shortly after the Decree on Peace.

November 1917: Decree on the Rights of the People of Russia. This claimed that peoples of the Russian Empire, throughout the old empire, had been treated badly and that the Bolsheviks would put that right.

In particular, the Decree stated that:

The united will of the Congresses and the Councils of the People's Commissars, has resolved to base their activity upon the question of the nationalities of Russia, as expressed in the following principles:

1. The equality and sovereignty of the peoples of Russia.
2. The right of the peoples of Russia to free self-determination, even to the point of separation and the formation of an independent state.
3. The abolition of any and all national and national-religious privileges and disabilities.
4. The free development of national minorities and ethnic groups inhabiting the territory of Russia.

Thus, for the national minorities, the Decree promised much and the expression of support for freedom, self-determination and independence suggested that, in theory, they would be much better off under communist rule. Reinforcement of such rights was provided in the first Russian constitution (see page 93) and there was little to suggest that the promises made would be reneged on.

Also by November 1917, Lenin had started to deal with the demands of war by introducing State Capitalism. This involved the state taking complete control of the economy until it could be 'safely' handed over to the proletariat. This was not part of a grand plan but simply a reaction to the crisis situation that the Bolsheviks faced. Nevertheless, it still fitted with (or was made to fit) Bolshevik ideology. State Capitalism was introduced by way of the following measures.

- November 1917: Decree on Land. This involved the seizure and division of private landholdings that were then handed over to peasants.
- November 1917: Decree on Workers Control. Workers' Committees were given 'extra' powers to run factories.
- December 1917: Formation of the Supreme Economic Council (SEC). The SEC was formed to manage key industries that were **nationalised** by the Bolsheviks.

This did not prevent 'local' nationalisation occurring via soviets. The nationalisation process was therefore tightened by two further decrees: one in the summer of 1918 and the other in the spring of 1919. These resulted in the nationalisation without compensation of all enterprises employing more than ten workers. The effect was to create over 30,000 nationalised economic entities by 1920 ranging from windmills to huge steel plants. The SEC soon struggled to cope with the management of this and was therefore soon made subservient to the more powerful Council of Labour and Defence, personally chaired by Lenin.

Lenin obviously believed centralised control of this nature was essential if Russia was to survive the effects of war. He also knew that it was likely to hasten the move towards full-blown civil war and the creation of further economic problems. From Lenin's perspective, a civil war might be welcomed as it provided an opportunity to defeat, once and for all, those who opposed what he was aiming to achieve.

Council of Labour and Defence

The Council of Labour and Defence was first established as the Council of Workers' and Peasants' Defence in November 1918. It was responsible for the economy, which included the production of military supplies. During the Russian Civil War, the council issued emergency decrees to maintain the production and supply of equipment and munitions for the Red Army.

Activity

This section has considered a number of ways by which Lenin began to consolidate Bolshevik power. It is important that you are aware of the significance of each factor in this consolidation and to do this you should be aware of the strengths and limitations of each issue so that you can make a judgement about their importance.

1 Use the chart table to help you. Give a score out of ten (ten being the highest) for the relative strengths and limitations of the measures mentioned. For each score explain your decision.

Method or factor used to consolidate Bolshevik power	Strength of the measure in increasing power	Limitation of the measure in increasing power
The establishment of the *Sovnarkom*		
Press restrictions		
Arrests		
Decrees		
Treaty of Brest-Litovsk		
National Minorities		
State Capitalism		
Council of Labour and Defence		

What were the causes and course of the Russian Civil War (1918–21)?

From the Spring of 1918 to the end of 1921, Russia was ravaged by a civil war. The most important question to be answered is the extent to which it was provoked and planned by the Bolshevik leadership.

The Russian Civil War was the result of Bolshevik actions and policy, opposition to Bolshevik rule and the will of some national minorities to break away from the control of a centralised Russian government. Also of importance were the effects of the First World War, especially on the living and working conditions of the populace. It is possible that 'ordinary' people associated a lack of food, clothing and shelter with the inability of the Bolsheviks to deal with the knock on effects of the war. Each of the groups of protagonists in the war is usually referred to by a colour:

- the Bolsheviks were the Reds
- political opposition groups to the Reds were the Whites
- national and regional minorities were the Greens.

Bolshevik actions and policies

The following actions and policies, either deliberately or not, provoked a major backlash against Bolshevik rule.

- The reforming decrees: these favoured the bulk of the population at the expense of the wealthy minority especially landowners and the business classes.
- The Treaty of Brest-Litovsk: the loss of land was resented by patriotic Russians.
- The shutting down of the Constituent Assembly and the subsequent centralisation of administration: liberals, SR and Mensheviks viewed this as the end of any prospect of democracy being installed.
- The suppression of opposition: the banning of parties, control of the media, the establishment of the *Cheka* (see page 87) and the use of the Red Army (see page 87) to prevent demonstrations reinforced the belief that one form of autocracy was being replaced by another.

> **The *Cheka***
>
> The term is short for 'The All-Russian Extraordinary Commission for Fighting Counter-Revolution, Sabotage and Speculation', a rather convoluted title for what was the secret police. Their main role at this time was to seek out and destroy those who were against the achievements of the October 1917 revolution. After the Civil War, the *Cheka* was disbanded and replaced by the State Police Administration (GPU) in 1922. The latter was expanded in 1924 and renamed the United State Police Administration (OGPU). Although OGPU was not as brutal as the *Cheka*, it still instilled fear in the general public.

Opposition

The main opponents of Lenin consisted of those who had come to reject the Bolshevik leaders' ideology and policies over the long-term as well as after the events of October 1917 to January 1918. Despite the repression adopted by the Bolsheviks, the Mensheviks, SR and liberals did not disappear: they found ways of regrouping to launch a counter attack on those they despised.

- After Kerensky fled the Winter Palace, on 25 October 1917, he went on to organise an army made up of eighteen Cossack companies to attack Petrograd. The former Provisional Government leader hoped the Cossacks would be supported by soldier cadets and officers left in the capital who were disenchanted with the Bolshevik coup.
- At the same time as the planned Petrograd assault, garrison forces in Moscow, sympathetic towards Kerensky, attacked Bolshevik officials and troops.
- In January 1918, a Union in Defence of the Constituent Assembly was formed in an attempt to protect the new democratic body; about 50,000 supporters gathered on the opening day of the Assembly to demonstrate their allegiance even though the Bolsheviks had banned public meetings.

These revolts and demonstrations are often seen as the start of the Civil War. Although easily put down by the Bolsheviks, they were an indication that further trouble was likely. By the Spring of 1918, opposition groups located on the borders of Bolshevik controlled territory had become entrenched. The stage for a full-blown civil war had been set.

The will of national minorities

A number of national minorities, especially the Ukrainians and Georgians, were keen to maintain the independence they gained through the Treaty of Brest-Litovsk. Their fear was that once the First World War ended, the Bolsheviks might attempt to take back the territory they had ceded. When the outbreak of civil war occurred, national minorities started to mobilise against the Bolshevik Red Army: there was a realisation that the war, coupled with the German defeat in the First World War, meant there would be a good chance of independence being lost. The minorities, in the form of Green armies, proved to be strong opponents of the Bolsheviks and were a major reason why the civil war was so prolonged.

The consequences of the First World War

By the time Russia was about to leave the First World War, it was clear that the Russian peoples had experienced immense suffering.

- A collapse of the transport system throughout Russia had led to a reduction in food supplies and a subsequent rise in food prices and starvation; by the end of March 1918, bread in Petrograd was being rationed at 50 grams a day (the lowest ever recorded level).
- Food shortages were made worse with the handing over of Ukraine, Russia's biggest grain producing area, to Germany under the Treaty of Brest-Litovsk.
- Workers left the main industrial cities for the countryside in search of food; this posed a major threat to the Bolsheviks as their main power base was in urban areas. In the first six months of Bolshevik rule, about 1 million workers migrated. The metal industries of Petrograd were very badly affected: from October 1917 to April 1918, their workforces had reduced by 80 per cent.
- Some entrepreneurial peasants had started to hoard foodstuffs, especially grain, as they could not buy much with the money they might gain from selling it.

Lenin responded to the living standards crisis by introducing War Communism (see page 86). How far this was a tool to benefit the whole population is a matter of great debate.

How did the course of the war unfold?

The fact that the Civil War lasted over four years gives testament to the scale and magnitude of the forces that were determined to overthrow Lenin and his comrades.

The chronology of the war suggests that it unfolded through a number of stages which, to an extent, overlapped. The stages should be interpreted and analysed by cross-referencing to the following two maps (see page 81 and 84).

The Green Armies

The armies of the Reds, in particular, during the Civil War were boosted by merciless conscription campaigns. Those who resisted were classified as deserters; under the Bolsheviks desertion was punishable by death. Deserters often fled to forests (hence the association with the word Green) to form armed bands that became known as Green armies. On occasion they acted independently but at other times they acted as militias for local peasant communities. After 1920, Green armies were generally linked with anti-urban views and represented the interests of national minorities as in the Ukraine. Also, they were involved in taking over and governing some of the major towns in parts of Russia notably Tobolsk and Petropavlovsk (both in Siberia).

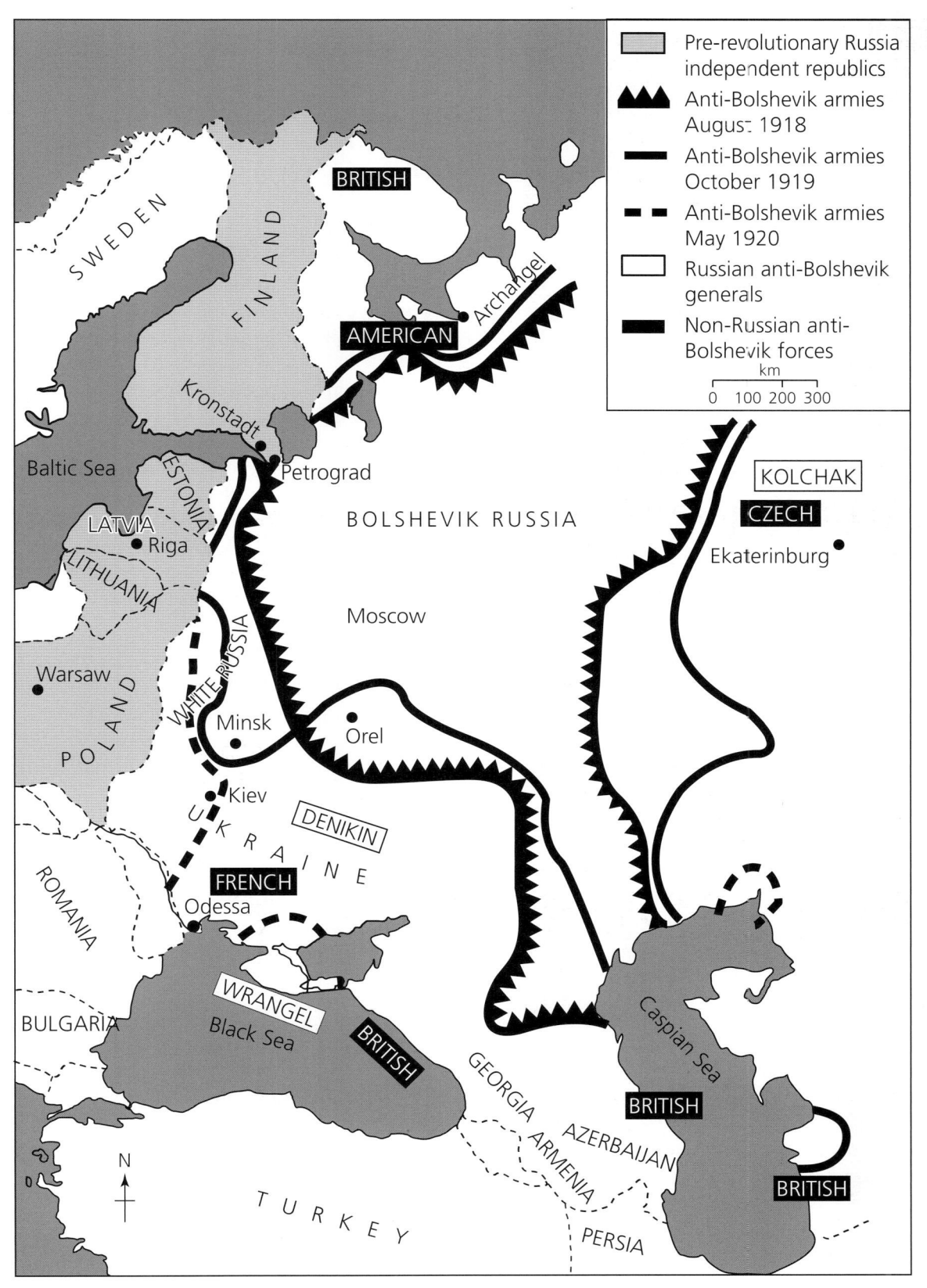

▲ The Civil War in Russia, 1918–20

The Czech Legion

After the Treaty of Brest-Litovsk a group of Czech and Slovak soldiers (the Czech Legion) found themselves stranded within Russian territory. During the First World War they had fought on the side of the Russians as they believed this would help their nations gain independence from the Austro-Hungarian Empire. When Russia withdrew from the war, the Legion decided to continue fighting against their enemy by relocating to France but to do this they realised they would have to circumnavigate the world by travelling east. At first the Soviet leaders were sympathetic and about 35,000 members of the Legion were given the authority to travel, armed, on the Trans-Siberian railway, to begin their journey. However, when they reached the Urals, local soviets were suspicious of the Legion and tried to remove their weapons. The legion broke up into smaller units and proceeded to attack towns protected by the Red Guards. Enemies of the Bolsheviks realised they might harness the support of the Legion by promising them external support from the French and British. This did result in foreign intervention on behalf of the Whites, although it played little part in determining the outcome of the Civil War. After November 1918, the end of the First World War, the Legion had little motivation to continue fighting: they disbanded and individuals attempted to find their way back to their homelands.

Stage 1: initial resistance

- Spring 1918: Opposition from Cossacks in the region of the Don and the Urals was nullified.
- April 1918: Having defeated General Kornilov's volunteer army in the Don region, Lenin proclaimed that the war was about to end. Foreign intervention occurred in this month when British marines were sent to support those opposing the Bolsheviks.

Stage 2: the strengthening of SR resistance

- May 1918: The Czech Legion on its way back to Vladivostok revolted and became a focus for those who wanted to add extra military muscle to their efforts against the Red Army. The SR, in particular, were keen to ally with the Czechs.
- July 1918: The Tsar and most of his family were executed by the *Cheka* at Ekaterinburg.
- August 1918: Trotsky signalled his intent in ensuring the cohesiveness of the Red Army by executing deserters. The Bolsheviks became concerned at the arrival of more foreign troops, this time from the USA.
- September 1918: The Directory government that emerged at Ufa was made up primarily of SR and Czechs. By this time, opposition fighting forces were known as the White armies.
- November 1918: Admiral Kolchak announced himself as Supreme Ruler (of the White armies).

On 4 July 1918, the ordinary guards for the royal family were replaced by those from the *Cheka*. The Ural Soviet suggested to Bolshevik officials in Moscow that they should be executed. On 12 July they received word that the central regime was happy for the Ural soviet to make the decision independently. Subsequently, on 16 July, all of the family members were either shot or bayoneted to death. The bodies were then abandoned in a disused mineshaft. The murder of the tsar should also be seen in the context of three other developments that were used to justify a reign of terror, of which the murder of the tsar could be seen as just one part:

- in July 1918, a group of SR members had assassinated the German ambassador in protest at the terms of Brest-Litovsk
- an attempt was made to kill Lenin on 30 August 1918, he was shot but survived
- the Petrograd chairman of the *Cheka* was murdered, also on 30 August.

The execution of the royal family without a trial can therefore be seen as part of the brutal way in which the government through the *Cheka* responded to any danger and allowed them to attack not just individuals but a whole class. This brutality was only added to by the Civil War, the social problems of famine and the threat to the survival of the Bolshevik party, which ensured that any criticism was silenced and that the 'enemies of the working class' were exterminated to save the Revolution.

▲ The Czech Legion during Russian Civil War

Stage 3: the Reds versus the Whites

- December 1918 to the end of 1920: White armies fought against the Reds. The Red Army, based mainly in Moscow, initially soaked up attacks from the Whites from all directions.
- October 1919 onwards: the Red Army scored notable victories over the Whites (for example, against General Deniken, leader of the White Volunteer Army, at Orel and against General Yudenich, leader of White forces made up of prisoners of war released by Germany, at Petrograd). By the depth of winter, the Red Army had started to advance.
- January 1920: Admiral Kolchak resigned (and was subsequently executed by the Bolsheviks). Certain regions, such as Ukraine, also demanded to be freed from central control, as they believed they should be allowed to develop a separate national identity. These regions constituted nationalist forces that created further difficulties for the Reds. By February, there were signs that the resistance from the nationalists was receding (for example, Estonia signed a peace agreement with *Sovnarkom*).
- November 1920: Red forces drove out the last of the White troops from southern Russia.

Stage 4: the Reds versus the Poles

- April 1921: Polish armed forces attacked Russia and reached as far as Kiev in the east. Russian forces counter-attacked and pushed the Poles back to Warsaw.
- Another counter-attack in August, this time by Poland, resulted in the Red Army retreating. The Russo–Polish conflict eventually came to a halt in March 1921 when the Treaty of Riga was signed.

Ekaterinburg and the murder of the tsar

When Nicholas II Russia abdicated, he and his immediate family were sent to Tobolsk in western Siberia, where they were treated fairly, but after the Bolshevik takeover, they were transported to a house in Ekaterinburg in the Urals. Once the Civil War got under way, it soon became evident that the White armies were in a position to capture Ekaterinburg and rescue the Romanovs — meaning that the tsar would then provide a figurehead for a counter-revolution before being restored to the throne.

The Directory government at Ufa

The Directory government was a counter-revolutionary organisation that was created by the Ufa State Conference on 23 September 1918, in Ufa (southern Russia). It brought together the Committee of Members of the Constituent Assembly and the Provisional Siberian Government (Omsk).

General Anton Denikin 1872–1947

Denikin was a former tsarist general who supported Kornilov.

General Nicolai Yudenich 1862–1933

Yudenich was a former tsarist general who had had a distinguished career, notably in the Russo–Japanese war.

Treaty of Riga

Under the Treaty of Riga Poland was allotted substantial amounts of land in Byelorussia and Ukraine; Russia did not regain this until 1939.

Russia 1894–1941

Legend:
- Curzon Line, proposed by Britain as Poland's eastern boundary, December 1919
- Polish armies, April 1920
- Extent of Polish advance June 1920
- Russian advance and retreat, July–September 1920
- Boundary of Poland and Russia established by Treaty of Riga, March 1921

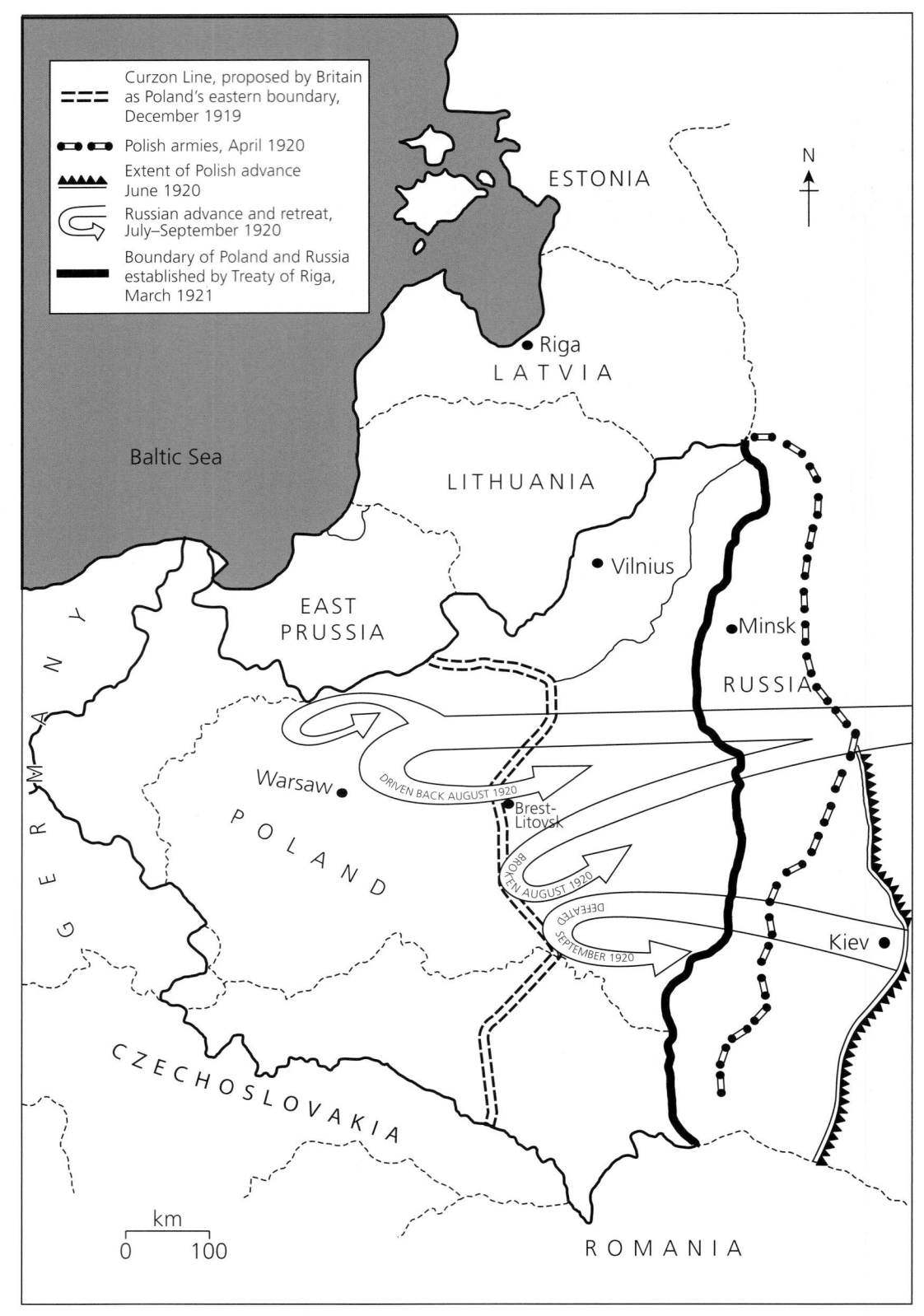

▲ Russian–Polish War, May–September 1920

Stage 5: end of the Civil War

- Throughout 1921, semi-independent peasant armies formed to oppose the Bolsheviks. Their aim was to gain more freedoms from Bolshevik leaders. The protracted war ended with victory for Reds but forced Lenin and his associates to reconsider the future path that Russia needed to take.

Activity

1 Using this section consider the following statements and find evidence to support or challenge them:
   - Lenin was responsible for the outbreak of the Civil War because of his bid for absolute authority.
   - The Civil War was simply a desperate struggle for food as the Bolsheviks failed to end hunger.
   - The Civil War was an attempt at revenge by a majority party, the SR, against a minority party, the Bolsheviks.
   - The Civil war was a class war.
   - The size of Russia meant that the Civil War was more about local and regional considerations than larger issues.
2 Which of these statements best explains the reasons for the outbreak of civil war? Explain your choice.
3 If you think there is a better explanation then write your own statement and provide evidence to support it.

Change to Why did the Bolsheviks win the Civil War (1918-21)?

By considering the preamble and course of the war (especially in terms of its geographical context) it is easy to understand why the Reds were victorious. The reasons are summarised in Table 2.

Table 2 Reasons why the Reds won the Civil War

Red strengths	White and Green weaknesses
Leadership	**Leadership**
Trotsky, acting as the Bolshevik war commissar, proved to be very skilful in managing the Red Army. No White leader matched Trotsky's strategy and tactics and his ability to sustain the morale of troops. Lenin was also instrumental in ensuring that Bolshevik supporters remained united in their belief in the socialist cause.	The White leaders struggled to co-operate and to co-ordinate their activities. This was partly caused by geographical separation but also as a result of not having a common set of aims. Some Whites were socialists while others were conservatives looking to restore some kind of aristocratic rule. There were also regional differences; some White (and Green) leaders viewed the Civil War as an opportunity to seek autonomy or even independence for their region.
Strategy and tactics	**Strategy and tactics**
Trotsky's strategy was based on maintaining lines of communication within the Red Army, breaking the supply lines to White army groups and preventing White army groups from co-ordinating their activity. Integral to the above strategy was the tactic of controlling and maintaining the railways, especially in the areas around Petrograd and Moscow. Trotsky and Lenin planned for links between the Red Army forces to be secured, to ensure the defence of Russia's two most important centres of industrial production and where the Bolsheviks had first consolidated their power. Once Petrograd and Moscow were deemed safe, the Red Army was then co-ordinated to go on the offensive, pushing back the White forces to the key frontlines.	The lack of a clearly defined, unified set of aims resulted in no coherent plan as to how the war could be won, neither was there any analysis of the most effective tactics to use. The urban strongholds of the Bolsheviks proved very difficult to penetrate and without much access to the railway system the Whites and Greens had little chance of co-ordinating their activities.

Red strengths	White and Green weaknesses
The other main tactic employed by the Bolsheviks was the imposition of *Cheka* brutality (see page 87). Without the *Cheka* it would have been difficult to have imposed the strict wartime measures (especially War Communism and the militarisation of labour), both of which were considered necessary for victory.	
Resources Both the Reds and Whites used conscription to boost their forces. Trotsky turned the 'Workers' and Peasants' Red Army' into a more professionally organised and disciplined Red Army. By 1920, Trotsky was managing over 3.5 million troops and at the end possibly as many as 5 million. Former tsarist military officers were also employed by the Reds to counter the experience of military leaders found in the ranks of their opponents. Similarly, Red cavalry units were formed to oppose the Whites use of Cossacks in the south. Although there were desertions from the Red Army, the Red Terror helped maintain cohesiveness. From the start of war, the Reds controlled the industrial centres in Russia and hence were able to quickly produce munitions to support the army.	**Resources** About 500,000 White soldiers were said to exist at any one point during the conflict; this was much less than the number deployed by the Reds. The Whites had to rely on foreign supplies of armaments.
Logistics By controlling the railways, the Reds were able to move troops and supplies over vast distances far more quickly than the Whites. Trotsky had his own armoured train constructed so that he could move from front to front in short periods of time. He supposedly travelled over 65,000 miles during the war!	**Logistics** The Whites found it hard to link their forces and some of the Green forces were little more than peasant bands.

What were the consequences of the Civil War?

For peasants and workers throughout the newly established Russian Soviet Federative Socialist Republic (RSFSR) (see page 93) and what was the old Russian Empire, the Civil War had very dramatic short- and long-term consequences. There was considerable suffering as a result of the Bolshevik measures used to direct the course of the conflict (most notably War Communism and the Red Terror). Once the war had ended, the population was then faced with fall-out of the Bolshevik victory.

War Communism

During the Civil War, Lenin used State Capitalism alongside grain requisitioning to create what was labelled War Communism. The key features of War Communism were the following.

- Nationalisation (state control) of larger enterprises and a state monopoly of markets for goods and services. The nationalisation of industry and state monopoly of markets caused unrest as it meant that individuals lost the freedom to produce and sell goods at a time, price and place that suited them. They lost all ownership and hence control over the means of production, distribution and exchange.
- Partial **militarisation of labour**. The militarisation of labour was also disliked as people were forced to work solely to meet the needs of the war.
- Forced requisitioning (taking) of agricultural produce. Grain requisitioning was the most hated policy as it involved taking away surpluses of food and grain, which meant there was a disincentive to grow more than was actually needed by an individual household. Often, the majority of food would be taken from a household to feed the army and urban workers. The overall result was famine in rural areas (especially between 1920 and 1921).

Famine

Starvation occurred owing to the combination of grain requisitioning, drought and the disruption caused by the Civil War. The harvests of 1920 and 1921 produced 50 per cent less than in 1913 and probably as many as one in five of the population was starving. The Bolsheviks accepted there was a major food crisis and accepted help from foreign food associations (especially the American Relief Association). Despite relief arriving in the form of US$60 million of food aid it is likely that by the end of the Civil War 5 million people had died as a result of the famine.

The Red Terror

Lenin believed that stability and cohesion in Russia could be achieved only through repressing, forcefully, those who challenged the underlying principles of his ideology, Marxism-Leninism (see page 92). He claimed that: '... coercion is necessary for the transition from capitalism to socialism. There is no contradiction between Soviet democracy and the exercise of dictatorial powers.' The coercion used by the Bolsheviks came in the form of the *Cheka* and the Red Army.

The *Cheka*

The *Cheka* was established by the Bolsheviks in December 1917, and headed by a Polish communist, Felix Dzerzhinsky. Their specific role involved dealing with counter-revolutionaries. By the summer of 1917 they began to clamp down on left-wing SR, especially after members of this group were linked with an attempt to assassinate Lenin in August 1918. The *Cheka* differed from previous variants of the secret police since they used terror to victimise people based on *who* they were, and not just because of their alleged actions. Thus, Dzerzhinsky instructed *Cheka* members that: 'Your first duty is to ask him to which class he belongs, what are his origins, his education, and his occupation. These questions should decide the fate of the prisoner.'

Under the guidance of Trotsky and Dzerzhinsky, the *Cheka* formally implemented the Red Terror. This involved enforcing War Communism (especially grain requisitioning), the **Labour Code**, the elimination of kulaks, the administration of labour camps and the militarisation of labour. After the Civil War, the *Cheka* was disbanded and replaced by the State Police Administration (GPU) in 1922.

The Red Army

Under the guidance of Trotsky, the Red Army was instrumental in enabling the Bolsheviks to win the Civil War. At the start of the war, the Red Army hardly existed, but by the end it consisted of over 5 million conscripts. In comparison, the White opposition could muster only about 500,000 troops. The army was also used to impose, along with the *Cheka*, War Communism.

The importance of the Kronstadt rising

Despite creating a more disciplined army, Trotsky faced problems of desertion, rebellion and a number of anti-Bolshevik risings in response to the requisitioning of grain. The most notable example was in February 1921 when sailors mutinied at Kronstadt (a naval base located on Kotlin Island just west of Petrograd). While the risings were confined to the peasantry they were less of a problem but when there was opposition within the party it was a serious problem. Petrograd workers crossed to the naval base at Kronstadt and joined the sailors and workers to demand more freedom.

The demands that the workers and sailors drew up were less of a concern to Lenin; it was the fact that it was done by the very people who had supported the Bolsheviks in 1917 that was the issue. Then, they had been seen as 'heroes of the revolution', now they threatened to destroy it. Trotsky ordered 50,000 troops to recapture the island; this was achieved with 10,000 Red Army casualties. The rebels who were captured were executed, or exiled to the Arctic. Lenin argued that the rising had been led by enemies of the revolution and therefore suppression was justified. However, this was far from the truth and was seen in the decision to lessen the harshness of War Communism and ultimately led to the introduction of the New Economic Policy, designed to end the famine and lessen opposition.

Felix Dzerzhinsky 1877–1926

A Polish communist who came out of exile as a result of the February Revolution. He was appointed as head of the *Cheka* (1917–26) because of his ruthlessness, reliability and dedication to the cause.

Kulaks

The Bolsheviks popularised this term to indicate the existence of a class of allegedly rich, exploiting peasants. Some historians point out that it was a term used after the 1861 Emancipation Edict and was derived from the Russian *Kulaki* (meaning 'fists').

Labour camps

Punishment camps where political opponents were set to hard labour. They were placed in the more inhospitable parts of Russia, such as Siberia.

Although there was a softening in terms of economic policy, it was not accompanied by a political one, and, if anything, Bolshevik control was actually increased.

The longer term consequences of the Civil War

Defeat in the Polish campaign brought a similar kind of humiliation to the Bolsheviks as the Russo-Japanese War did to Nicholas II. Once again, a Russian army was defeated by another army, which, on paper, was vastly inferior. Coupled with this, foreign intervention during the war on behalf of the Whites and a general mistrust of the Bolsheviks by Western European governments put Lenin on the defensive. Although **Comintern** and the concept of **world revolution** were not abandoned, the Bolshevik government moved towards a foreign policy centred on developing peaceful relations.

The war influenced the nature of Russian government in so far as victory had been achieved through a particular kind of discipline, administration and management. The post-war communist government consisted of men who had served in the Red Army, the *Cheka* and other bodies. This experience was carried over into the running of the new Russia. The emphasis was on orderliness, trustworthiness, comradeship and loyalty to the party. The militaristic approach to government is well illustrated by the introduction of War Communism (see page 86). The effects of this, along with the actions of the *Cheka*, caused divisions within the party and a move away from the use of 'terror' to control the populace.

The Civil War largely nullified any positive impact that State Capitalism might have had. Industrial output in a number of sectors fell dramatically. For example, the production of coal fell from 29 million tonnes in 1913 to 8.9 million tonnes in 1921. Inflation was such that the rouble by October 1920 was worth only 1 per cent of its 1917 value. This resulted in the virtual abandonment of the currency so that, for example, 90 per cent of all wages paid to workers by the start of 1921 were **in kind**. Some services, such as tram rides, were free as it was impossible to pay for them. On top of this, millions were starving as a result of the famine of 1920 to 1921. Such a drastic situation clearly required a change of approach. The New Economic Policy (see pages 89–90) was introduced to bring stability to government even though it appeared to be in contradiction of all that the communists stood for.

It is also fair to say that the war led to power being even more centralised than before. Power revolved around the Politburo and Orgburo (see page 76). This meant that these very tightly knit party sub-committees became the main organs of government.

Activity

The key issue to consider is why the Reds won the Civil War and whether victory was due to Red strengths or White weaknesses. Although an exam question might ask you why the Whites lost, it would still require you to use the same information.

1 For each of the following factors explain how it helped the Bolsheviks win and then assess the importance of each factor so that you can place them in rank order of importance. Having done this, write a paragraph explaining your order.
- Geographical factors
- Unity and Organisation
- Leadership
- Support
- Foreign Intervention
- Propaganda

How significant was the New Economic Policy (NEP)?

Why was the NEP introduced?

By 1921, workers, peasants and party members were clamouring for something 'new' to address the hardships caused by both the First World War and the Civil War. It is debatable as to how far Lenin viewed War Communism as a short-term emergency measure but he was quick to change tack and replaced it with his New Economic Policy (NEP). More specifically, the NEP was introduced to:

- solve the food crisis that had emerged in Russia; the harvests of 1920 and 1921 had produced less than 50 per cent of that achieved in 1913; also, Lenin had, reluctantly accepted foreign aid especially from the USA via the American Relief Association (ARA)
- quell the possibility of further out breaks of resistance, such as that which had occurred at Tambov (1920–21) and Kronstadt (see page 87)
- show that Lenin was both pragmatic and flexible in his thinking – before introducing the NEP he claimed that:

'There must be a small amount of freedom for the small private proprietor … the effect will be the revival of the petty bourgeoisie and of capitalism … We must not be afraid of Communists "learning" from bourgeois specialists, including merchants, small capitalist co-operators and capitalists.'

Lenin issued the decree on the NEP in the spring of 1921.

What was the NEP?

The key features of the NEP were as follows.

- Denationalisation of small-scale enterprise and a return to private ownership. This was to allow small workshops to flourish to produce consumer items such as clothes and shoes.
- The continuation of the state control of heavy industry but through the use of trusts. These organisations were to pay strict attention to accounting procedures and were responsible for the purchase of raw materials and equipment and the payment of wages.
- Rejuvenation of trade through the removal of restrictions on the private sales of goods and services. Shops flourished, rationing was ended and a new, revalued rouble was introduced.
- A return to the encouragement of foreign trade, investment and the import of foreign expertise.
- An end to grain requisitioning and a return to peasants being allowed to sell surpluses in local markets.

What were the consequences of the NEP?

The short-term impact was impressive. Industrial output increased rapidly and this was reflected in the greater amount of food and consumer goods found in shops and markets (see Table 2). This was linked to the emergence of a new breed of entrepreneur, the Nepman. By 1923, Nepmen were responsible for over 60 per cent of retail trade but they had already started to anger people with their methods.

Tambov

In Tambov peasant armies were formed and they attacked the requisitioning squads and took over considerable parts of the countryside. They were able to raise some 20,000 men and the Red Army struggled to regain control.

Petty bourgeoisie

This is a term that refers to those of a lower (small) middle class consisting of part-independent peasantry and small-scale merchants who aspired to become part of the higher middle classes.

Nepman

A nepman was a 'new' type of businessman that emerged as a result of the NEP (wealthier peasants, retailers, traders and small-scale manufacturers). They stood to gain from the free trade allowed under NEP: fewer restrictions on what, when and where to trade meant greater profits.

▲ A poster promoting the NEP: 'From the NEP a Socialist Russia Shall Emerge', 1930, artist Gustav Klutsis

Another cause for concern by that time was the emergence of what Trotsky called the 'Scissors Crisis'. It was called this as graphs depicting falling agricultural and rising industrial prices looked like a pair of scissors.

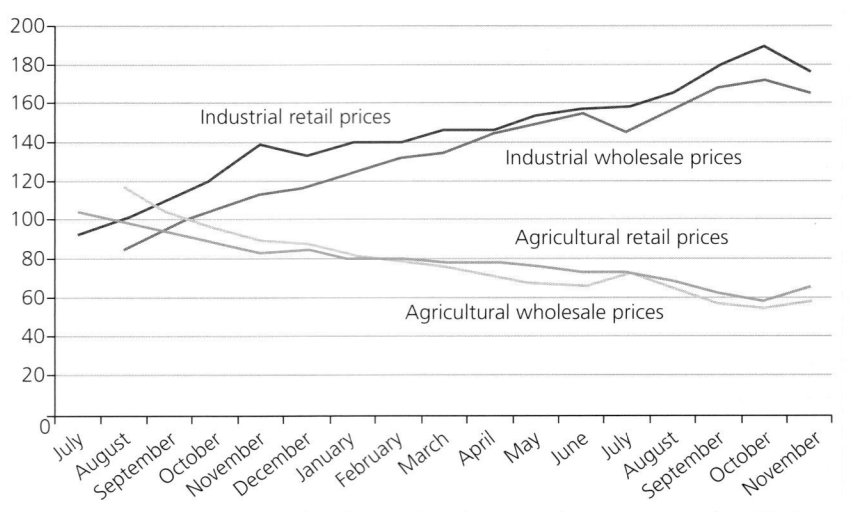

▲ The Scissors Crisis: industrial and agricultural prices, July 1922–November 1923

The supply of food increased at a rate that far exceeded domestic demand, resulting in a swift fall in prices. In comparison, the supply of manufactured goods increased at a much slower pace, which left prices relatively high. Peasants were therefore reluctant to sell surpluses at low prices but the frustration was that industrialists needed them to do this so that they could afford to buy their products. As the historian J.N. Westwood has pointed out, this was 'less serious than it seemed at the time' as it was relatively short lived.

Table 3 Russian agricultural and industrial production, 1921–26

	1921	1922	1923	1924	1925	1926
Grain harvest (millions of tonnes)	37.6	50.3	56.6	51.4	72.5	76.8
Sown area (millions of hectares)	90.3	77.7	91.7	98.1	104.3	110.3
Industrial (factory) production (millions of rubles at 1926–27 value)	2,004	2,619	4,005	4,660	7,739	11,083
Coal (millions of tonnes)	8.9	9.5	13.7	16.1	18.1	27.6
Electricity (millions of kilowatt-hours)	1,945	775	1,146	1,562	2,925	3,508
Pig iron (thousands of tonnes)	116	188	309	755	1,535	2,441
Steel (thousands of tonnes)	183	392	709	1,140	2,135	3,141
Cotton fabrics (millions of metres)	105	349	691	963	1,688	2,286
Rail freight carried (millions of tonnes)	39.4	39.9	58.0	67.5	83.4	–*

Note: *Data not available.

Source: A. Nove, *An Economic History of the U.S.S.R.*, Allen Lane, 1969, page 94.

As with War Communism, the NEP was promoted by the Politburo as 'a temporary deviation, a tactical retreat'. In other words, Lenin saw the NEP as a measure to help the Russian economy get back on its feet by stimulating production of goods and services. It also appeased sectors of society who had opposed the stringency of War Communism.

Despite this, debate raged over the extent to which the NEP was a betrayal of the October Revolution and communist ideals. This was partially resolved with a demand for political unity after the fright of the 1921 Kronstadt rising (see page 87). With the death of Lenin, though, in 1924, and the ensuing power struggle, the divisions within government widened and centred on the effectiveness of the NEP. Those in favour of continuation were known as the Rightists (right opposition) and those that opposed were called the Leftists (left opposition). During this time, Stalin remained fairly ambivalent about the NEP, but as the longer term effects of it were felt he became a major critic. This coincided with him taking the leadership in 1929 and it was not long before he abandoned the NEP and created the Great Turn.

Activity

In studying the NEP, it is important to consider two main issues. First, the extent to which it was different from War Communism and, second, how successful it was.

1 Complete the following two tables to (a) explain the similarities and differences between War Communism and the NEP and (b) to access the success of the NEP. You will need to refer to the previous chapter to enable you to complete the task in full.

How similar were War Communism and the NEP?

Factor	War Communism	NEP
Obtaining grain from the peasantry		
Large-scale industry		
Small-scale industry		
Private trading and ownership		
Transport		
Banking		

How successful was NEP?

Issue	Evidence of success	Evidence of failure
Upholding Communist ideology		
Increasing agricultural production		
Increasing industrial production		
Gaining support among the Bolshevik party		
Gaining support among the workers		
Gaining support among the peasantry		

How successful was the creation of the new communist government and the constitutions?

The main way in which the success of the new communist government and the constitutions can be measured is by considering the extent to which the aims and objectives behind each political and governmental reform, as expressed through communist ideology, were met.

Russia 1894–1941

> **Marxism-Leninism**
>
> Marxism-Leninism was Lenin's interpretation of Marxism, which argued that the move to worker control of the means of production, distribution and exchange could be speeded up.

Ideology

After the October Revolution of 1917, Lenin began to implement Marxism-Leninism. Opposition to Bolshevik ideology and rule had resulted in the Russian Civil War. Some historians have argued that Lenin welcomed the war as an opportunity to eradicate the bourgeoisie. Although the Bolshevik Reds defeated the Whites this did not safeguard Marxism-Leninism. Within the party, debate continued over strategy. Lenin's toleration of the 'moderates' was evident when he replaced War Communism with the NEP. War Communism was associated with famine, whereas the NEP was more liberal and gave the people freedom to produce goods and services without limited restriction (see page 89). More radical members of the party criticised these 'bourgeois' concessions, and demanded more central control. Others, such as Trotsky, pushed for a move towards a 'Permanent Revolution', which entailed spreading communism throughout the world and not just Russia. Trotsky's views were criticised by Stalin who preferred a policy of establishing 'socialism in one country'. Stalin argued that the Communist Party could not influence the growth of communism elsewhere until it was firmly established within the Soviet Union.

These developments influenced Lenin to adjust his ideology and policies to stave off opposition, but he had no intention of veering away from his short-term goal of ruling, with the help of the party, as a dictator. His initial policy of appeasement did not fully resolve the issue of opposition within the ruling elite. It took a far more radical approach to do this.

The Bolsheviks promoted the party as one that was working to create an egalitarian society based on democratic centralism. Central control of Russian affairs would be in the hands of politicians elected by the Russian people (that is, the people of the RSFSR).

However, all key government posts were held by senior Bolsheviks, and the administration was swamped with the **leading cadres** of the Bolshevik Party. During the Civil War, any opposition towards a one-party state was eradicated, often with the help of the *Cheka*. Anyone wanting to be involved in politics either had to get permission to join the Bolshevik Party, or else become part of an opposition movement in exile.

> **Democratic centralism**
>
> Under the Bolsheviks, the people would agree to being led by a cadre (group of key personnel) based in Moscow, until a genuine workers' government could be put in place.

As the party essentially became the government, membership of the former was increasingly seen as a privilege and a way to become more socially mobile. Thus, membership numbers grew significantly during the immediate post-Civil War period. In 1921, there were around 730,000 members, but by 1928 this had increased to about 1 million. Many found new careers and opportunities as part of the *Nomenklatura*, but the role of members depended mainly on their socio-economic background. By the time of Stalin's accession to power, the party had become very hierarchical.

- By the early 1930s, nearly 10 per cent of the party were made up of *apparatchiki* (full-time, paid party organisers). These were educated members of society who served mainly as party secretaries.
- About 30 per cent of the party were employed as 'other' administrators. These too were educated people who, under the tsarist regime, had largely been part of the growing middle class.
- The rest of the party consisted of workers and/or peasants who, in their spare time, operated as party activists.

As the party and government became more centralised and nepotistic, the political regime became less democratic. Officials became more detached from grassroots affairs, and workers showed less interest in politics.

This was reinforced by the changing nature of the proletariat. More industrial workers were recruited from the ranks of the peasantry who were notorious for being apathetic towards party affairs. Recruitment campaigns such as the **Lenin Enrolment** attempted to address the issue, but they had minimal effect on the composition of the party.

Constitutions

Two major constitutional changes were made during Lenin's rule. First, the constitution of 1918 created the Russian Soviet Federative Socialist Republic (RSFSR). The new republic was made up of Russia and parts of central Asia, most notably Kazakhstan, Uzbekistan and Turkmenia. Second, the 1924 constitution formalised and developed stipulations made under a treaty of 1922. The Republics of Ukraine, Belorussia and Transcaucasia joined with the RSFSR (thus forming the United Soviet Socialist Republic or USSR, the official title of the Soviet state after 1922). Each republic was allowed its own government and other symbols of sovereignty such as national flags. However, such governments were still answerable to *Sovnarkom*. Hence, Russia remained firmly a one-party state.

Activity

This section has focused on the creation of the new Bolshevik government and the constitutions.

1 You need to be able to assess the success or otherwise of these developments and reach an overall judgement. Use the table below to help you do this.

Issue	Evidence it was a success	Evidence it was a failure	Mark out of six: 0 = failure; 6 = very successful	Judgement

2 Use the information in the chart, from this section and further research to help you plan an answer to the question: 'How successful were the Bolsheviks in establishing a new government in the period from 1917 to 1924?'

To what extent was Lenin a strong leader of the Bolsheviks?

How Lenin's strengths and weaknesses are viewed is likely to depend on how sympathetic one might be to what he was trying to achieve and how he went about fulfilling his aims. Also, Lenin had different strengths and weaknesses according to the role he played – as a member of the intelligentsia, party leader or leader of Russia.

Strengths

- Lenin was a 'conviction' politician. Throughout his career he stuck to his belief that the imposition of Marxist ideas was the only way for a more just, fair and equal society to come about in Russia.
- Despite his Marxist convictions, Lenin was also flexible in his thoughts and actions. For example, he initially believed that a revolution in Russia could be achieved only with the support of workers and not peasants. When peasants started to show 'revolutionary behaviour', such as seizing land from the nobility, Lenin changed his mind and acknowledged that rural protesters had an important role to play in political change.
- Lenin's self-belief proved invaluable in helping him deal with opposition.
- When Lenin experienced what others would have seen as setbacks, such as being exiled, he saw these as opportunities.
- Fellow Bolsheviks displayed much loyalty towards their leader, even when they disagreed with him. This suggests Lenin's intellectual abilities coupled with his pragmatism were admired and respected.
- Lenin was an opportunist; he knew when to take advantage of the weaknesses shown by his opponents, especially the Mensheviks and the Provisional Government.
- Above all, Lenin was a person of great intellect. He was adept at converting some of the more abstract ideas of Marxism into something that could be understood by workers and peasants. In response to the context he found himself working in, he developed his own ideology of Marxism-Leninism.

Weaknesses

- Lenin used considerable force, with the resultant human casualties, if it meant he was to achieve his aims. Generally, Lenin could be seen as much of an oppressor as the tsars (hence, he, along with Stalin has been referred to as a 'Red Tsar').
- Lenin was so single-minded about Marxism that he refused to accept that there were possible alternatives to achieving a more just society. This caused opposition to him gaining momentum, including within his own party.
- Opposition to Lenin also strengthened when he banned other political parties.
- Lenin's economic, social and political reforms could be seen to have set Russia backwards, but much depends on how the costs and benefits of capitalism are viewed, as opposed to those of Communism.

Politically, Lenin's strengths outweighed his weaknesses. He was clearly a talented politician but this needs to be measured against some of the methods he used to achieve his political goals. Lenin was so narrow minded and obsessed with making political gains that he lost sight of the moral implications of the level of repression that he deployed.

When Lenin died in 1924, he was held in total reverence by party members. Anyone who could demonstrate, at that time, that they were totally in line with Lenin's thinking and were willing to continue with the policies he had set out would have had a good chance of assuming his mantle.

Activity

In many ways this chapter has focused on the role of Lenin, with this last section providing a summary of his strengths and weaknesses. It is important that you have a clear understanding of these, but it might also be helpful to think about the extent to which Lenin changed the course of history in the period from 1917 to 1924, this will involve you re-reading this chapter and the last parts of the previous chapter.

1 Complete the table below to help you assess his role.

Event	Lenin was responsible	Other factors were responsible
The April Theses		
The October Revolution		
The establishment of a one-part state		
The Treaty of Brest-Litovsk		
The creation of the Red Army		
Victory in the civil war		
War Communism		
New Economic Policy		

2 Use the information in the table and from the section above to help you plan an answer to 'How significant a contribution did Lenin make to the establishment of the Bolshevik state?'

Historical debate

Ideology or circumstance: which shaped the nature of Bolshevik rule?

The key debate about this period concerns the extent to which circumstances, rather than Bolshevik party ideology shaped the nature of Bolshevik rule. Some have argued that that it was the extreme situation in which Russia found itself between 1917 and 1924 that led to the terror, while others have argued that it was Lenin's belief in the dialectical process that explain the severity of repression that was seen in these early years of Bolshevik rule.

Passage 1

Whatever the pre-revolutionary attitude of the Bolsheviks to democracy in and outside the party, to free speech, civil liberties and toleration, the circumstances of the years 1917–1921 imposed an increasingly authoritarian mode of government on and within a party committed to any action that was or seemed necessary to maintain the fragile and struggling Soviet power. It had not actually begun as a one-party government, nor one rejecting opposition, but it won the Civil War as a single-party dictatorship buttressed by a powerful security apparatus, and using terror against counter-revolutionaries. Equally to the point, the party itself abandoned internal democracy. The 'democratic centralism' which governed it in theory became mere centralism.

Eric Hobsbawm, *Age of Extremes*, 1994

Russia 1894–1941

Activity

1. In light of the two passages and further research, do you agree with the view that it was 'the circumstances of the years 1917–1921 that led them [the Bolsheviks] to adopt an authoritarian mode of government'?
2. Using the information in this chapter, find evidence to support each of the two views.
   - It was the pressures of Civil War that led the Bolsheviks away from democracy after it took power.
   - It was Lenin's belief in the dialectical process that led to the severity of repression in the years 1917–24.
3. Which of the views do you find more convincing? Explain your choice.

Passage 2

Historians debate the extent to which the party-state came into being as the result of ideology or the pressure of civil war. Some argue that the seeds of Bolshevik tyranny lay in the Marxist notion of the dictatorship of the proletariat; others in Lenin's notion of the vanguard party with its implication that the party knew what was best for the working class. Yet the civil war was as much about certain principles being jettisoned as about others being confirmed. The fact that ideology evolved in this way suggests that it was not the sole or even paramount driving force behind the creation of the party dictatorship. If the seeds of dictatorship lay in ideology, they only came to fruition in the face of the remorseless demands placed on party and state by civil war and economic collapse. The Bolshevik ethos had always been one of ruthlessness, authoritarianism and class hatred, but in the context of civil war these qualities transmogrified into cruelty, fanaticism, and absolute intolerance of those who thought differently.

Steve Smith, *The Russian Revolution*, 2002

Further research

Martin Gilbert, *The Routledge Atlas of Russian History*, Routledge, 2007

Geoffrey Hosking, *Russia and the Russians: from Earliest Times to 2001*, Penguin, 2001

Christopher Read, *Lenin*, Routledge, 2005

Robert Service, *A History of Modern Russia: From Nicholas II to Putin*, Penguin, 2003

Geoffrey Swain, *Russia's Civil War*, History Press, 2008

Ian Thatcher, *Trotsky*, Routledge, 2003

J.N. Westwood, *Endurance and Endeavour: History 1812–2001*, Oxford University Press, 2002

Chapter takeaways

- A constituent assembly eventually met but lasted only one day. It was closed with the use of force indicating both Lenin's disdain for the Assembly but also the degree of threat he felt it posed to the continuation of the Bolsheviks.
- Once Lenin had gained power, he had the task of consolidating it. He did this through the promise of reforms (in the form of decrees) and the use of repression (secret police and the Red Army).
- The Russian Civil War was caused by, on the one hand, opposition to the Bolshevik taking of power but, on the other, Lenin's willingness to let such a conflict take its course. Lenin seemed to will the war so that he could eliminate his enemies once and for all.
- The Bolsheviks won the Civil War due to superior leadership and human resources. However, their opponents were disorganised and un-coordinated.
- Lenin was quick to replace War Communism, deemed necessary to succeed during the Civil War, with the NEP. The NEP appeased, to an extent, those who suffered under War Communism but was not accepted by all members of the Bolshevik party.
- By 1924, under a number of constitutions, a new communist government was established. It seemed successful in that economic and social stability was achieved in Russia. However, the government was tainted by factional infighting that came to the fore when Lenin died in 1924.
- Lenin was undoubtedly a skilled politician and was strong in the sense that he showed a strong conviction towards Marxist ideology and the belief that this would lay the platform for a more just and equitable society. However, his main weakness might be that he resorted to force.

Study skills: Avoiding descriptive answers, writing analytically and the crucial importance of the opening sentence of each paragraph

The types of question set for AS and A Level essays will be the same and therefore all the advice in this section applies to both examinations.

Avoiding descriptive answers and writing analytically

What is meant by a descriptive answer? This is when an answer has relevant supporting knowledge, but it is not directly linked to the actual question. Sometimes the argument is implicit, but even here the reader has to work out how the material is linked to the actual question. Instead of actually answering the question, it simply describes what happened.

In order to do well you must write an analytical answer and not simply tell the story. This means you must focus on the key words and phrases in the question and link your material back to them, which is why the plan is crucial as it allows you to check you are doing it. You can avoid a narrative answer by referring back to the question as this should prevent you from just providing information about the topic. If you find analytical writing difficult, it might be helpful to ensure that the last sentence of each paragraph links back directly to the question.

Consider the following question:

> **Example**
>
> **'The most important feature of the Civil War was the emergence of War Communism.' How far do you agree?**
>
> In order to answer this question you would need to consider the following issues about the Civil War and War Communism:
>
> - the motives for War Communism
> - the features of War Communism that made it an important tool
> - the contribution of War Communism to Bolshevik success.
>
> Then you would need to consider other factors such as:
>
> - the role of the *Cheka*
> - the role of the Red Army
> - the links between War Communism and the *Cheka* and Red Army.
>
> A very strong answer will weigh up the relative importance of each factor as it is discussed, a weaker answer will not reach a judgement until the conclusion, and the weakest answers will either just list the reasons or, worst of all, just describe them.

Russia 1894–1941

The following is an extract from a sample descriptive answer for the question above:

> **Sample answer**
>
> War Communism was probably the most important feature of the Civil War for three reasons. First, it involved nationalisation (state control) of larger enterprises and a state monopoly of markets for goods and services. Second, it led to the partial militarisation of labour, which was disliked as people were forced to work solely to meet the needs of the war. Third, forced requisitioning (taking) of agricultural produce occurred as a result of War Communism. This was the most hated policy, as it involved taking away surpluses of food and grain. War Communism was therefore important but there were other features of the Civil War that stood out, particularly the Red Terror.

This paragraph simply lists the main features of War Communism albeit in some detail. It does not get to grips with the thrust of the question; it has not explained the relative importance of War Communism with respect other factors such as the *Cheka* and Red Army. It needed to explain why War Communism was so important to Lenin and the Bolsheviks but also how it could not have worked without the use of repression in the form of the secret police and armed forces.

The opening sentence of each paragraph

One way that you can avoid a narrative approach is to focus on the opening sentence of each paragraph. A good opening sentence will offer a view or idea about an issue relevant to the question, not describe an event or person. With a very good answer you should be able to read the opening sentence of each paragraph and see the line of argument that has been taken in the essay. It is therefore worth spending time practising this skill.

> **Question practice**
>
> In order to practise the skill of directly answering the question, write six opening sentences for the following essays.
> 1 Assess the reasons for the Bolshevik victory during the Civil War.
> 2 'The most important result of the NEP was the stimulus given to internal trade.' How far do you agree?

> **Short answer essay question**
>
> Which was the more important factor in enabling the Bolsheviks to win the Civil War?
> (i) Trotsky
> (ii) The Cheka
>
> Explain your answer with reference to (i) and (ii).

> **Activity**
>
> **How successful was the New Economic Policy (NEP)?**
>
> Look at the following eight opening sentences. Which of these offer an idea that directly answers the question above and which simply impart facts?
> 1 The NEP was very successful insofar as it increased industrial production.
> 2 The NEP created nepmen.
> 3 In the short-term, the benefits of the NEP were reflected in increased grain production: the harvest went up from 37.6 tonnes in 1921 to 76.8 tonnes in 1926.
> 4 By 1923, nepmen were responsible for over 60 per cent of retail trade.
> 5 Despite the gains for nepmen, the NEP was not seen as beneficial by those who thought there was too unscrupulous dealing that was resulting in higher than necessary prices for manufactured goods.
> 6 The NEP was flawed as it led to the Scissors Crisis.
> 7 The Scissors Crisis did not detract too much from the success of the NEP as it was only a short-lived phenomenon.
> 8 Under the NEP, peasants were reluctant to sell surpluses at low prices.

The rule of Stalin

This chapter analyses the rule of Stalin up to the start of the Great Patriotic War, which began when Germany invaded the USSR and therefore covers the impact of the first two Five Year Plans. Stalin's character and abilities are assessed with reference to how he first won the power struggle after Lenin's death and then how he proceeded to consolidate his authority. The rivalries and divisions in the Bolshevik party are analysed by considering the interactions between Stalin, Trotsky, Bukharin, Kamenev and Zinoviev. Particular attention is given to the debate over the principles of 'socialism in one country' as opposed to that of 'permanent revolution' as this was at the heart of the disagreements between Soviet factions. An assessment is then made of the tools Stalin used to strengthen his position, which includes a consideration of his use of propaganda and the 'cult of personality', the police state, purges and gulags. The last part of the chapter considers the important area of economic policy in the late 1920s and throughout the 1930s; there is still much controversy over the level of success obtained by Stalin with respect to his industrial and agricultural strategies and its high cost in human terms. The chapter addresses a number of key questions.

- Why is it important to consider Stalin's character and abilities when assessing his rise to power and policies?
- How important was the role of rivalries and divisions within the Bolshevik party in Stalin's rise to power?
- How effective was Stalin's use of propaganda and censorship in consolidating power?
- How effective was Stalin in creating a police state?
- How successful were Stalin's agricultural policies in the 1930s?
- How successful were Stalin's industrial policies in the late 1920s and 1930s?

The chapter will also consider the study skills of writing a conclusion and overall essay writing. It will explain the need to reach a supported judgement, which is based on the argument and view offered in the rest of the essay. The section will consider how to weigh up factors and reach a judgement about the relative importance of factors and the approach to be taken when the question puts forward a named factor as the most important reason.

Timeline

1924–25		Stalin publicly attacks Trotsky for being unfaithful to 'Leninism'
1925	December	Allied with Bukharin and the 'Rightists', Stalin begins attacks on Zinoviev
1926	October–November	At the Fifteenth Party Congress, Stalin attacks the 'United Opposition' of Zinoviev, Kamenev and Trotsky
1927	November	Kamenev and Zinoviev expelled from the Party; Trotsky expelled and sent to Central Asia
1928		Introduction of the first Five Year Plan
1929	April	Stalin begins attack on Bukharin
	November	Bukharin removed from the Politburo
	December	Stalin announces 'liquidation of the kulaks as a class'; collectivisation begins in earnest
1931–32		Terrible famine across the Soviet Union; millions die
1934	December	Murder, by Stalin's agents, of Sergei Kirov; beginning of 'Great Terror'
1935	January	Zinoviev, Kamenev and others are arrested, accused of complicity in Kirov's assassination

Russia 1894–1941

1936 August	First 'show trial': Zinoviev, Kamenev and their allies confess and are executed
1937 January	Second show trial
1937 June	Purge of the army; top generals are tried and executed
1938 March	Third show trial, conviction and execution of Bukharin and Rykov among others
1939 March	At Eighteenth Party Congress, Stalin announces end of the Great Terror
August	Nazi–Soviet Pact is signed in Moscow
September	Outbreak of Second World War
1940 August	Trotsky assassinated, by Stalin's agents, in Mexico City
1941 June	Hitler invades Soviet Union

Overview

After Lenin died in 1924, a power struggle ensued between Stalin, Trotsky, Kamenev and Zinoviev. Through skilful manipulation of grassroots party members Stalin was able to build enough support to outmanoeuvre his rivals and take control, in 1927, of the Bolshevik Party Congress. By doing this he effectively became the new leader of Russia. His rivals continued to oppose him but he eventually got rid of them through the execution of Kamenev and Zinoviev, and the assassination of Trotsky.

Stalin roughly translated means 'man of steel'. This says much about Stalin's character and abilities as he revealed a level of hardness and ruthlessness that instilled fear throughout Russian society. Stalin used his tough approach to centrally plan the economy. In 1928, the first Five Year Plan was introduced and a year later he brought in the first wave of rural collectivisation. Both measures were aimed at raising production and **productivity** so that Russia could be seen as being as economically powerful as its Western counterparts (the USA, Britain, France and Germany). His initial economic policies seemed to achieve their objectives but at a considerable human cost; those who chose or who were unable to work in the new system were severely punished.

Stalin's economic policies were enforced through the creation of a police state. The *Cheka* was replaced by the United State Police Administration (OGPU), which in turn was taken over by an even more fierce form of secret police, the Commissariat for Internal Affairs (NKVD) in 1934. The secret police became the main organ of government used to terrorise the people into submitting to every whim of the Russian leader. Although there was a thaw in repression from 1933 to 1934, this was followed by a period called the Great Terror when Stalin's perceived enemies in government were put on show, tried, exiled or executed. By 1939, Stalin was in a very powerful position.

In 1939, Stalin signed a Non-aggression Pact with Nazi Germany. This was partly signed to give Russia time to, ironically, prepare for war against Germany, which the Soviet leadership viewed as inevitable. The economic gains of a second Five Year Plan (1933–37) were supplemented, in 1940, with other industrial measures, such as the direction of labour to prepare for invasion. The invasion was eventually repelled (1944–45) and Stalin continued as leader, now in a virtually impregnable position, until his death in 1953.

Why is it important to consider Stalin's character and abilities when assessing his rise to power and policies?

One of Stalin's leading biographers, the historian Robert Service, has claimed that Stalin had 'a gross personality disorder', that is, a personality that was not predictable. This may or may not have been true but it is important to make some attempt to assess the character and abilities of Stalin insofar as they affected his decision making. This can be done without labelling Stalin as a madman and without making value judgements about his character.

Character

Stalin is often depicted as a schemer and obsessive in wanting to gain personal power. His megalomania or hunger for power seems to have gone hand-in-hand with psychopathic tendencies, especially later in his career when he instigated the Great Terror (see page 111). This was fuelled by paranoia; Stalin increasingly believed that no-one was to be trusted, including loyal party supporters and members of his own family. However, the view of Stalin as a madman has recently been challenged by the historian Stephen Kotkin. He believes that Stalin was far more diligent, intelligent, resourceful and rational than has often been made out. Like Lenin, he was a conviction politician who adhered to the tenets of his own brand of Marxism (Marxism-Leninism-Stalinism).

Abilities

Stalin showed many abilities as a Bolshevik Party member and, later in his life, as leader of communist Russia. He was a competent administrator, manager, and planner of strategy and resources. As general secretary of the Communist Party in 1922, and then as leader of Russia, Stalin showed he could manipulate situations to serve his wants and needs. These were not simply based on selfishness; they can be viewed as an attempt to modernise Russia from within, while protecting it from external threats.

Stalin as an administrator

The following are examples of how trusted Stalin could be as an administrator.
- In 1905, Stalin represented local branches of the Bolshevik Party, Georgia and South Russia, at conferences.
- In 1912, Stalin was elected to the Central Committee of the **Bolsheviks** where he excelled as an administrator and debater.
- Before 1917, Stalin had responsibility for raising funds for the party, albeit through illegal means, such as bank hold-ups and train robberies. Up to this time, Stalin had been arrested on eight occasions and sentenced to time in prison and exile.

Stalin as a manager

Stalin was given extra responsibilities after showing his skill as a member of the Central Committee.
- From 1917 to 1922, Stalin was the Bolshevik specialist manager of national minorities' issues, having been appointed commissar for nationalities in the first Soviet government.
- Stalin's management skills were also evident in the role he played as a military commander during the **Civil War**.
- As general secretary of the Communist Party Stalin held the most senior of all management posts.

As a manager of people, Stalin was adept when dealing with those involved in the power struggle after Lenin's death, especially Trotsky, Kamenev and Zinoviev. By 1927, Stalin controlled Party Congress, which allowed him to expel his main rivals from the party.

Stalin's more sinister management of people can be seen through the instigation of the Great Terror, the show trials of 1936–38 and the appointment of Lavrentiy Beria as head of the secret police.

Stalin as a planner

Stalin planned economic and social change, linking this with target-setting in an attempt to modernise Russia and improve its standing as a world power. This was reflected in:

- the introduction, from 1928 to 1933, of a planned economy and the police state; in 1928, the first Five Year Plan was adopted (see page 118)
- the start of the collectivisation programme in 1928 (see page 113)
- managing Russia's resources from 1939 to 1941, to prepare for a possible Nazi invasion.

By January 1924, Stalin had worked himself into a position of power by exploiting the key administrative post, as general secretary, which he held. He could not have reached this position through luck. He had the ability to plan, organise and implement his ideas effectively. This was evident in the way he become leader of Russia and in how he implemented his plans to modernise Russia. However, Stalin also had the ability to be ruthless when he deemed it necessary. He used an unprecedented level of repression when faced with what appeared to be intractable issues, such as Lenin's legacy, a stagnant economy, opposition from national minorities and a changing world political climate.

Collectivisation

A communal system of faming whereby peasants shared resources to produce food, which was then distributed to ensure that local populations were adequately fed. Surpluses were sent to urban populations.

Activity

1 Read the following statement about Stalin's character and abilities. What kind of historical evidence would you need to prove that the personality traits mentioned were true?

'Stalin had a narcissistic personality, characterised by his total self-absorption and his conviction that he was a genius' (Alan Bullock, 1991).

Personality trait	Evidence
Narcissistic (excessive interest in himself)	
Self-absorbed (selfish or self-centred)	
Conviction he was a genius (deluded about abilities)	

2 Use the information from this section to support or challenge the following statements, then as you study each section in the book return to these statements and add further evidence to either support or challenge the views that Stalin:
- was an able administrator
- was a loyal party member
- had an aptitude for planning especially when it came to economic affairs
- was a conviction politician; he stuck closely to Marxism-Leninism-Stalinism.

How important was the role of rivalries and divisions within the Bolshevik party in Stalin's rise to power?

Under Lenin, there were a number of occasions when internal disagreement threatened to derail the revolutionary movement. Disagreements soon turned into strong rivalries. The main party leaders involved were Trotsky, Nikolai Bukharin, Kamenev, Grigory Zinoviev and Stalin. Lenin had little option but to direct the actors so that the revolution stayed on course and no individual attempted to change the gains made from the revolution. Although rivalries had always existed in the Bolshevik party, they became more evident after the Bolsheviks gained control of the government in 1917 and were revealed in a number of different ways.

- After the overthrow of the Provisional Government in 1917, a number of prominent Bolsheviks, including Kamenev, Zinoviev and Alexei Rykov, called for a coalition to be formed with other socialist groups. Although some left-wing SR were allowed to join the ranks, Lenin bullied his Bolshevik colleagues into rejecting an alliance with opposing political groups.
- The signing of the Treaty of Brest-Litovsk (see page 77) was opposed by the left, especially Trotsky. Lenin countered his opponents by claiming Germany would be defeated in the First World War and that it would soon be over; he stressed that the territorial losses resulting from the Treaty would be reversed. However, not all Bolsheviks were convinced by this argument
- The adoption of War Communism (see page 86) during the Civil War was considered harsh by some party members. Lenin conceded to pressure for change and introduced his NEP (see pages 89–90). This heightened tensions and widened divisions. Right Bolsheviks favoured this temporary concession towards capitalism, while left Bolsheviks saw it as a betrayal of revolutionary principles.

The prelude to the power struggle

Lenin's failing health before 1924 started a 'power struggle'. There were three key developments before Lenin's death in January 1924. First, a clique called the Triumvirate (*Troika*) was instigated within the Politburo, consisting of Zinoviev, Kamenev and Stalin. Its purpose was to combat the growing influence of Trotsky, whom Lenin seemed to favour as a successor. Then, in December 1922, Lenin provided his Political Testament, a document that criticised the personal attributes and achievements of many leading Bolsheviks. Stalin received heavy criticism for how he ran **Rabkrin** and his role in the 1921 'Georgian Affair'. However, by January 1924, Stalin had worked himself into a position of power by holding various political posts, including that of general secretary. As the historian Chris Ward has indicated, by the time Lenin's health started to deteriorate, Stalin was '… the only leader who was simultaneously a member of the Politburo, Orgburo, Secretariat and Central Committee. In addition, he could look back on almost seven years' experience of military commissions and jobs in the state's embryonic administrative apparatus.' This partly explains why Stalin took over the mantle from Lenin with relative ease.

Nikolai Bukharin 1888–1938

Bukharin joined the Bolshevik Party in 1906 and soon became an ally of Lenin. He developed his career as a leading Bolshevik theorist, using *Pravda* to promote his ideas. In 1922, the so-called 'golden boy' of Lenin's regime became a full member of the Politburo.

Grigory Zinoviev 1883–1936

Zinoviev rose to prominence as chairman of the Petrograd Soviet (1917) and later chairman of **Comintern** (1919–26). He was a close colleague of Lenin, since 1903 and the founding of the party. He was executed in the purges under Stalin.

Alexei Rykov 1881–1938

Rykov was chairman of the Central Committee of the CSPU and served as prime minister from 1924 to 1930.

Georgian Affair

The mishandling of Georgian nationalism, in 1922, by Grigol Ordjonikidze, the Commissar for National Affairs in Georgia. Ordzhonikidze (supported by Stalin) believed that Georgia, Armenia and Azerbaijan should be amalgamated but leaders of the Georgian communist party disagreed. In a meeting over this Ordzhonikidze physically attacked one of the leaders resulting in condemnation by Lenin. Stalin, however, defended his friend's actions.

Ideological divisions and the power struggle

After Lenin's death, the manoeuvring for power intensified, which highlighted the factions that existed within the party. At this point, leading Bolsheviks disagreed over three key policy issues:

- there was much dispute between left and right Bolsheviks over whether there should be a continuation of the NEP
- many demanded that a more openly democratic form of government should be adopted
- the link between ideology and the future of communism caused much consternation. The left, under the guidance of Trotsky, continued to press for a Permanent Revolution, while the right emphasised the need for Socialism in One Country. Stalin displayed skill in manipulating debates and individuals to consolidate his position, and thereby paving the way for a personal dictatorship.

Stalin's split with Zinoviev and Kamenev

The *Troika* successfully discredited Trotsky who, in January 1925, was replaced as commissar for war. It is often said that Trotsky's former allegiance to the **Mensheviks**, his manner and his popularity in the army alienated opponents, some of whom may have resented him as a Jew and a more cosmopolitan figure than some of the other leaders.

However, Kamenev and Zinoviev became concerned with Stalin's plan for dealing with peasants and with his foreign policy. They verbally attacked Stalin but with little success; both were removed as local secretaries of the Party. The Politburo was simultaneously expanded (from six to eight members) and reinforced with Stalinists.

The United Opposition group

Trotsky, Kamenev and Zinoviev responded by forming the United Opposition group. Their opposition to the NEP and demands for more 'free speech' were treated with contempt. All were excluded from the Politburo. By 1927, Trotsky was expelled from the Party, and after continuing to provoke trouble was exiled to Kazakhstan. In January 1929, he was expelled from the USSR altogether.

The proposals for collectivisation

Stalin's proposals for collectivisation (see pages 113–14), including renewed grain requisitioning, were opposed by those on the right, who thought it resembled aspects of War Communism. Bukharin was particularly vocal in expressing his concerns and, as a result of joining forces with Kamenev, was branded a **factionalist**.

Other factors in the rise to power of Stalin

It was not just rivalries and divisions within the party that allowed Stalin to rise to dominance. Stalin was an astute politician and able to manipulate the situation following the death of Lenin to his own advantage, particularly in the defeat of his major rival, Trotsky.

Socialism in One Country

Socialism in One Country referred to the process of spreading and embedding socialism in Russia so that it could become strong and powerful from within. It would, through socialist policies such as the state control of economic institutions, become self-sufficient and less vulnerable to external ideological influences, such as capitalism. Stalin, and others, could not see how a Permanent Revolution could be established unless it was preceded by Socialism in One Country.

Permanent Revolution

The theory of Permanent Revolution was Trotsky's main contribution to the Bolshevik's interpretation and extension of Marxism. Trotsky argued that the Revolution of October 1917 would not be complete with the overthrow of bourgeois rule by the **proletariat**. It would need to continue on a national and international scale. At national level, completion would occur only with the total 'liquidation of all class society'. Completion internationally would happen with the 'final victory of the new (communist) society on our planet'. Trotsky did not think communism could survive in Russia against foreign countries, such as America, Britain, France and Germany, whose ideologies were based on free-market capitalism. It was never clear how Permanent Revolution could be achieved. This paved the way for an alternative view, pushed foremost by Stalin, of Socialism in One Country.

- Stalin suppressed **Lenin's Testament**, which made a number of critical comments about his person that would have been very damaging for him if it had been made public.
- Stalin took advantage of Trotsky's absence from Lenin's funeral to make the major speech and appear to be the 'true disciple of Lenin'.
- His role as leading mourner at Lenin's funeral suggested a continuity between Lenin and Stalin, which appealed to many.
- He used his position as general secretary of the Party to become indispensable in distributing patronage and put his own supporters in the top positions. As they owed their place to him they supported him in committees.
- Stalin used the **Lenin enrolment** that was designed to increase party membership to his advantage. Those who joined were aware that the privileges gained by joining the party depended on being loyal to those who had invited them to join and these were usually members of the Secretariat who Stalin controlled.
- Stalin took advantage of the attack on factionalism, which condemned party divisions and this made it difficult to criticise any decisions and allowed him to use it to attack any attempts at criticism.

However, it was not just Stalin's strengths that allowed him to emerge triumphant, but he was undoubtedly aided by failings and weaknesses in Trotsky.

- Trotsky was viewed with suspicion by many in the party as he had been a former Menshevik, joining the Bolsheviks only in 1917.
- Trotsky continued his holiday rather than attending Lenin's funeral. Initially, he claimed he had been given the wrong date but that was not true.
- Trotsky failed to take important jobs when offered, declining the post of deputy chairman of the Soviet government. He claimed that his Jewish background would embarrass the party, but he disliked mundane jobs and this prevented him from building up a following in the Party.
- Many in the Party feared that after Trotsky's success in the Civil War he would use the Red Army to establish a military dictatorship. Others feared his intellectual skills and therefore preferred to back Stalin who seemed less of a threat.

Outcomes

In 1929, Bukharin was ousted from his position as President of the Comintern editor of *Pravda*, and a leading member of the Politburo. Tomsky and Rykov also suffered demotions. Stalin simply gained the agreement of a core of loyal party members in order to remove 'critics' from positions of power. Thus, with both the left and the right removed from key jobs, Stalin was free to dominate proceedings. Both collectivisation and a series of Five-Year Plans (see pages 118–20) were implemented with a great deal of speed. Stalin's dominant position did not end criticism, but 1929 probably marks the point when it is difficult to distinguish between real and imaginary challenges to Stalin's authority.

> **Mikhail Tomsky (1880–1937)**
>
> Minister responsible for representing (in reality, controlling) the trade unions in Russia.

Russia 1894–1941

Activity

This section has focused on the reasons why Stalin was able to rise to power and dominate the Bolshevik party by 1929. Many examination questions ask you to assess the reasons for his rise to dominance and therefore it is essential that you have considered the role of a range of reasons.

1 Complete the table below to help you assess possible reasons.

Factor	Explanation of role	Mark out of six: 0 = no importance; 6 = great importance	Judgement
Control of the party organisation			
Stalin's personal skills			
Weakness of opposition			
Stalin's belief in 'Socialism in One Country'			
Stalin appeared to be the true disciple of Lenin			
Lenin's Testament			
Trotsky's weaknesses			

How effective was Stalin's use of propaganda and censorship in consolidating power?

Stalin used propaganda to promote a cult of personality and his polices of collectivisation and the Five Year Plans. Underpinning this was the intention of reducing opposition by the socialisation of Russians to worship Stalin so as to retain and maintain the dictatorial regime. Censorship was integral to this process as it prevented any verbal and written dissent.

▲ Propaganda posters from 1930s extolling (left) 'The victory of socialism in the USSR is guaranteed', artist Gustav Klutsis, and (right) 'We are on our way from industrialisation to socialism at full-speed', artist Mechislav Dobrokovsky

What tools were used to promote the cult of personality?

A variety of propaganda tools were used to promote Stalin's cult of personality most notably posters and associated slogans, newspapers, radio, film reels, groups, the arts, movements and leisure pursuits.

Posters and slogans

Propaganda posters appeared everywhere during the Stalinist era: in workshops, factories, schools, on street hoardings and on buildings. They aimed to inspire the people to work hard and to make sacrifices for the good of all. Some offered general messages while others were targeted at promoting particular Stalinist initiatives, such as industrialisation and the Five Year Plans (see the posters on page 106).

Newspapers

Under the communists, the main newspapers, *Pravda* and *Izvestiya*, were primarily propaganda tools rather than news outlets. Stalin used them to good effect to promote the need for, and achievements of, the Five Year Plans. Thus, for example, in 1932, *Pravda* reported that:

> The basic political task of the second Five Year Plan is the final liquidation of capitalist elements and of classes in general, the complete extermination of causes which tend to create class distinctions and exploitation, and the conquest of the remnants of capitalism in the economy and in the consciousness of the people; the transformation of the whole toiling population of the country into the conscious and active building of a classless socialist society. The proletariat of the USSR is in possession of absolutely all the possibilities, all the power, all the means and all the resources for the victorious fulfilment of this gigantic plan of construction of a socialist society.

How many ordinary Russians would have had access to such writings is unclear. *Pravda* was aimed mainly at party members. However, posters such as the ones on page 106 and the use of propaganda films did reach a wider audience.

Groups

Special youth organisations were established, the Pioneers and *Komsomol*, to protect the young against the 'degeneracy of bourgeois culture'. Komsomol was first established under Lenin but was formalised under the control of the Communist Party of the Soviet Union (CPSU) in 1926. The organisation was characterised by:

- being open to 14- to 28-year olds (there was the Young Pioneer movement for those under 14)
- members swearing oaths of allegiance to Stalin and the Party
- the provision of a route to full membership to the CPSU.

Komsomol members were encouraged to inform on those who criticised their leaders. Membership increased fivefold from 1929 to 1941. Most members were encouraged to support, with their labour, Stalin's economic projects. They also provided flag-wavers and cheerleaders used in May Day parades and the celebrations for Stalin's birthday.

Cult of personality

A cult of personality develops through the use of propaganda to build a positive image of a leader so that the population offers total obedience to that person.

The American writer John Steinbeck claimed, after a visit to Russia in 1947, that: 'Everything in the Soviet Union takes place under the fixed stare of the plaster, bronze, drawn or embroidered eye of Stalin.' The notion that Stalin was omnipresent (everywhere) and omnipotent (all powerful) is reinforced by thousands of eye-witness accounts such as that of Alexander Adeyenko, a steelworker, who stated that: 'Day and night radio told us that Stalin was the greatest man on earth — the greatest statesman, the father of the nation, the genius of all time.'

Both of these observations illustrate how Stalin's personality was constantly projected on to the people so that they would automatically obey his commands. Stalin soon developed, like Lenin, a following of unquestioning admirers that could be deemed to have been cult-like.

These types of accounts suggest there was no escaping the messages being put across about Stalin's greatness. However, there is also the possibility that many Russians genuinely liked and supported Stalin and that the propaganda messages were simply reinforcing what they already believed. This makes measuring the effectiveness of propaganda challenging.

The arts

The arts were manipulated to present a popular culture that emphasised the role of the 'little man' or the worker, traditional values, the community and the power of the state. Murals of collective farms were constructed and grandiose, gigantic buildings built. Any trends that veered from the norm, such as jazz music, were banned. Other, more classical art forms that reflected 'socialist realism', such as the music of Shostakovich, were encouraged and promoted.

The Stakhanovite movement

Propaganda was used in the workplace to raise productivity. The best example of this was the creation of the Stakhanovite movement. The movement was based on the extraordinary efforts of the Donbas miner, Alexei Stakhanov, who supposedly produced 100 tonnes of coal in a five-hour shift, which was fourteen times the required quota. He was turned into a 'model' worker for others to copy. Those who did were given special rewards, such as red carpets and holidays in Moscow. Although this achievement was used as propaganda to encourage other workers it actually created more problems as groups established to copy his achievement were given privileged access to tools and supplies and this disrupted plans and led to an overall loss of production where Stakhanovite movements were the strongest.

Leisure

Leisure pursuits were also targeted to promote communist ideals. The Dynamo and Spartak Moscow football teams were used to show the rest of Europe how successfully Russian people could perform under Communist rule. The Russian film industry began in 1907, and by the time of the October Revolution of 1917, there were over 1000 cinemas. By the late 1920s, Stalin was using the cinema to promote collectivisation and his Five Year Plans. Films, such as Sergei Eisenstein's *October*, were used to portray the 1917 Revolution as a popular rising. Under the guidance of the Council of People's Commissars, Soviet cinema was immersed in 'socialist realism'.

Censorship: socialist realism and the New Soviet Man

Socialist realism

Under Stalin, censorship was increased. By 1932, all literary groups were closed down and anyone wanting to write had to join the Union of Soviet Writers. During the first congress of the group in 1934, it was announced that members had to produce material under the banner of 'socialist realism'. This involved writing to depict the struggle of ordinary people to overcome oppression. Any work had to be approved by the Party. Some writers, such as Boris Pasternak, changed their beliefs to fit in with the wishes of the Union of Soviet Writers. Others rebelled and were arrested, sent into exile, or to labour camps or executed.

The New Soviet Man

A high degree of censorship continued during the Second World War. Stalin was especially concerned with doctoring information about the rest of the world. Radio broadcasts were distorted, news was fictionalised and restrictions were put on all of the arts to prevent bourgeois behaviour. Writers were still valued highly as the 'engineer of men's souls' (Stalin) but only if

---

Sergei Eisenstein 1898–1948

Eisenstein worked initially with the Bolsheviks in the Moscow Workers' Theatre before becoming a film producer. He produced a number of films that were used to promote the regime. First, *Strike*, made in 1924 showed how the workers were oppressed, followed by *Battleship Potemkin*, in 1925, and his most famous film, *October*, in 1928. It was a joke in the industry that more damage was caused to the Winter Palace and more people killed in its filming than in the actual Revolution, however it upheld the heroic myth of the revolution by the people.

they focused on glorifying Russia's achievements and promoted the concept of the New Soviet Man, who was the ideal Soviet citizen, hardworking, law abiding, moral and supportive of the Communist Party.

In summary, Stalin's uses of propaganda were very effective in that there was an apparent high level of support for his policies. However, it is difficult to be certain how many people were totally persuaded by the propaganda; conforming to Stalin's rules and regulations and worshipping him as an idol may have resulted more out of fear than a genuine love for the leader and the motherland.

> **Activity**
> 1. Make a list of the propaganda and censorship methods used by Stalin to consolidate his power.
> 2. For each one explain how they contributed to his consolidation of power.
> 3. Which do you think was the most important? Explain your choice.

How effective was Stalin in creating a police state?

Stalin's use of force as part of a police state was clearly effective in terms of achieving the desired result of eliminating most, if not all, opposition. However, it is possible that his opponents could have been kept in check using less violent means. There is also the view that having opposition in politics is healthy as it ensures that a given leader is forced to adopt policies that are in line with the general consensus. This masks the view that from Stalin's perspective there could be no challenge to his authority and criticism of his policies as that would have indicated a betrayal of what he, and Lenin, represented; the achievements of the 1917 revolution. Stalin, therefore, did not flinch from using force in a variety of forms to consolidate his power.

The growth of the police state: OGPU and NKVD

In a police state the role of the police is enhanced beyond normal day-to-day law enforcement, that is, according to guidelines that citizens understand and do not restrict their basic rights. In a police state a government tends to use the police to strengthen its authority with very strict law enforcement, which is often arbitrary and restricts basic rights, alongside the monitoring of the general behaviour of the population. Stalin believed that combining the use of ordinary and secret policing was crucial in ensuring that Soviet citizens obeyed his rules and in creating a sense of fear about what might happen if they were not compliant. This was tantamount to terrorising the population and it proved a highly effective way of preventing opposition from developing.

The United State Police Administration (OGPU)

After the Civil War, the *Cheka* (see page 87) was disbanded and replaced by the State Police Administration (GPU) in 1922. The latter was expanded in 1924 and renamed the United State Police Administration (OGPU). Although the OGPU was not as brutal as the *Cheka*, it still created fear in the general populace. The OGPU would take unsuspecting people from the streets for no obvious reason other than the fact they may have looked suspicious or that someone had reported their supposed anti-party behaviour. The OGPU, like the NKVD (see below), would often call on people at odd times, especially the early hours of the morning, arrest them and take them away for interrogation. Confessions of guilt were often extracted from people even though they may have been innocent of alleged crimes against the state. This was done to set an example and generally create fear.

The People's Commissariat for Internal Affairs (NKVD)

To combat opposition to Stalin's personal dictatorship, the NKVD (the People's Commissariat for Internal Affairs) was formed in 1934. Headed by Genrikh Yagoda, and later Nikolai Yezhov, the NKVD created a permanent structure of terror. It was crucial to the imposition of purges (see below), and was notable for gathering evidence against high-ranking communists, such as Bukharin, Kamenev, Zinoviev and Trotsky. The NKVD also helped administer the **Gulag** camps; over 40 million people were sent to these labour and prison camps during the Stalinist regime. However, Stalin suspected the NKVD of conspiracy. In 1938, Yezhov was blamed for an anti-purge campaign. He was replaced by Beria, who proceeded to arrange the execution of Yezhov and his close allies. By the start of the Second World War, the NKVD itself had been purged of around 20,000 members.

The military

The use of the military to help implement economic policy was furthered by Stalin. The Red Army was again required to requisition grain, this time as part of collectivisation. It also helped administer the purges, and played a role in the Great Terror. Ironically, the military leadership was consistently perceived as a threat by Stalin. He therefore removed a number of key military figures in the Great Purge of 1936–38, including the great Civil War hero, Marshal Tukhachevsky. By the end of the purge, over 40 per cent of the top echelon of the military had disappeared. This seemed illogical given rising international tensions following the Nazi seizure of power in 1933, and Hitler's expansionist foreign policy. In this way, Stalin's ambivalence towards the military could be seen to have hindered it as an effective tool for control.

Show trials

Another way used by Stalin to engender fear was through the use of show trials. These were trials in front of a public audience, although the audience would have been carefully selected by other Party officials. There were three major public trials that involved 'Left Oppositionists', who were mostly older Bolsheviks, being openly accused of a range of misdemeanours against Stalin and the USSR.

1. The murder of some of Stalin's close allies, most notably Sergei Kirov, and the perceived plotting to overthrow the Soviet leader himself resulted in the first major Stalinist show trial of August 1936. Fifteen of the sixteen accused were found guilty, having been forced into making confessions and were shot. On top of this, their confessions implicated others, especially Bukharin, Tomsky and Rykov, but after expressions of concern from those very close to Stalin, especially Ordzhonikidze, the accused were let off.
2. A second major show trial took place in early 1937. Experienced Bolsheviks such as Radek and Pyatakov were among the seventeen accused of working with Germany and Japan to plan the division of the USSR between the two and of sabotage and wrecking in general. This time thirteen were killed and the remainder sent to gulag camps where they subsequently died.
3. In March 1938, the last of the major show trials occurred. Among the 21 accused were Bukharin, Rykov and Yagoda. Their supposed crimes ranged from conspiracy to subvert the ruling regime, spying on behalf of external enemies and plotting to kill Lenin in 1918. Most followed the fate of those previously put on trial and were executed.

Genrikh Yagoda 1891–1938

Yagoda was a secret police official who rose to be head of the NKVD from 1934 to 1936. He was involved in the show trials of the 1930s and supervised the construction of the White Sea canal, built using slave labour. However, he was demoted as head of the NKVD in 1936 and arrested in 1937, charged with wrecking, espionage and Trotskyism. After his confession at his trial he was shot.

Nikolai Yezhov 1895–1939

Yezhov was known as the 'poisoned dwarf' because of his small stature and vicious behaviour. He was made head of the NKVD in 1937, but was later tried and shot.

Lavrentiy Beria 1899–1953

Beria held a variety of roles, including state security administrator, chief of the Soviet security and NKVD, becoming deputy premier in 1941 and a member of the Politburo in 1946. He played a crucial role in intelligence and sabotage operations on the Eastern Front in the Second World War, attended Yalta and helped to organise the takeover of state institutions in Central and Eastern Europe. He outlived Stalin, but was arrested on charges of treason during Khrushchev's coup. He was executed in 1953.

Mikhail Tukhachevsky 1893–1937

Tukhachevsky was a leading military commander and theorist from 1918 until his death. He commanded the Western Front against the Poles in 1920–01 and was chief of staff of the Red Army from 1925 to 1928. He played a key role in the modernisation of the Soviet army and helped to develop the theory of deep operations. He was accused of treason during the military purges of 1937–38 and shot.

The significance of the show trials was that:
- they showed that, according to the historian J.N. Westwood, 'there seemed little hope of resisting Stalin's forcefulness'
- by naming, shaming and implicating, the show trials had the desired effect of adding to the terror that was being created through the other modes of repression
- by 1930, most of the old Bolshevik party had 'disappeared'; 80 per cent of the membership in 1939 had been members only since 1930.

The show trials may have proved integral, and therefore effective, in helping create the Great Terror (see below) but they also caused much consternation among reactionaries in other countries who were not oblivious to the fact that trials were a facade. This was something of a problem for Soviet leaders as it painted them in a bad light and raised the possibility of Russia losing allies in a struggle against external threats such as Germany.

Purges: the Great Terror

Throughout the 1930s, there was a change of policy: critics ceased to be removed from key political posts, and were instead removed from the Party altogether. This is what is said to have been at the core of the so called Great Terror. According to J.N. Westwood, purging involved:

> ... thorough cleansing, and was used quite naturally to describe the periodic weeding out from party membership of those characters deemed unfit. From this small beginning the word came to describe a monstrous process of arbitrary arrests, fake trials, mass executions, and forced labour camps, which the weak and unlucky could not survive.

The purges of the 1930s were characterised by the following.
- Party members who failed to implement collectivisation adequately, or who disagreed with Stalin's attempt to 'liquidate the *kulaks* as a class' (see pages 116–17), lost their Party card, reducing total membership by about one-tenth.
- During the mid-1930s, the Party shed a further third of its members who were seen to be resisting the pace of industrialisation and collectivisation.
- From the mid-1930s, some prominent Politburo members were exiled or executed after being called oppositionists (see the section on show trials above).

By the beginning of the Second World War, however, Stalin's paranoia over those he believed to be challenging his authority had receded. In his mind he had achieved a major objective. Any internal opposition to Stalin had been eliminated and not just displaced. Internal opposition was more limited in scope and achievement during Stalin's rule than at any other time in the communist era.

Gulag camps

The Gulag (Main Administration of Corrective Labour Camps) organised a series of labour and prison camps. Similar camps had existed in the time of the tsars and Lenin but under Stalin they increased significantly and were deemed instrumental to the achievement of industrial and agricultural production targets. However, they were considered equally important as

Sergei Kirov 1886–1934

Kirov had been a prominent Bolshevik leader. He progressed through the Communist Party ranks to become head of the party organisation in Leningrad. On 1 December 1934, Kirov was shot and killed by a gunman at his offices in the Smolny Institute. Some believe his assassination was ordered by Stalin who was concerned by Kirov's growing popularity, even though he was purportedly a favourite of the leader, and organised by the NKVD, although the evidence for this is not clear-cut. Kirov's death served as an excuse for Stalin's escalation of repression against dissident elements of the Party, and disarming of the Party (every Party member was issued with a revolver up to that time). This was linked to the Great Purge of the late 1930s in which many of the Old Bolsheviks were arrested, expelled from the party, and executed.

Karl Radek 1885–1939

Radek had been a leading Bolshevik propagandist since 1905 and had been head of Cominern in the 1920s. He was part of the group accused of being Anti-Soviet Trotskyist Centre and also of spying.

Georgy Pyatakov 1890–1937

Pyatakov was an economist who had held government posts in the 1920s and 1930s. Like Radek he was accused of being a member of the anti-Soviet Trotskyist centre.

Liquidate the *kulaks* as a class

Stalin's policy to eliminate wealthier peasants (*kulaks*) as part of the class war in the countryside. *Kulaks* were considered to be bourgeois.

institutions of punishment for a range of crimes from the telling of jokes about Stalin, theft (especially of grain), murder, wrecking, sabotage and conspiracy.

The largest and most notorious camps were constructed in the most inhospitable parts of the USSR ranging from the Arctic north to Eastern Siberia and Central Asia. Inmates were forced to engage in hard labour, largely unskilled and manual, and to live in unsanitary accommodation. Women were especially badly treated: they were subject to mental and physical abuse, including rape. If they gave birth in the camp the child was invariably taken away and placed in a special orphanage. Hours of work were long, with 14 hours per day being the norm, conditions appalling and disease rife. This, combined with very basic food rations, led to high mortality rates. It has been suggested that by 1941 the forced labour system engaged about 3,350,000 prisoners, although this included 1 million or so placed in 'special settlements' who were often families of kulaks or other dissidents. At the end of the Great Terror, the annual death rate in Gulag camps was 91 per thousand but this increased to 170 per thousand during the period of the Second World War.

Gulag camps were an essential part of the Great Terror, being:
- places no-one wanted to be sent given the limited chances of survival
- another dimension to the repression, based primarily on trial and execution. In the peak years of the purges, 1937–38, around 780,000 executions were carried out
- a 'spin off' for the Soviet leadership in that they acted as hubs for industrial activity at no cost; Gulag camp inmates who withered away were easily replaced by a new wave of prisoners.

Thus, Gulag camps were part of a package of highly repressive tools used to stamp out opposition. From Stalin's perspective they were a very effective way of disposing of those who posed a threat while also sending a warning message to those who may have considered challenging his authority.

In summary, Stalin's police state was effective in that he retained power for a considerable period of time and with little overt opposition. It allowed him to implement his economic and social policies, although how beneficial these were is a matter for debate. The use of force on such a large scale came at the expense of the lives of millions of Russians. Stalin, and possibly more so, those who were close to him, were convinced that such human losses were necessary if a truly communist society was to be established. Those who lost their lives were simply seen as betrayers of the revolutionary ideals; those left were destined to lead to a society that would be better for the greater good. However, this clearly went against what many, then and now, would see as humanitarian concerns. It is difficult to understand from a non-Stalinist viewpoint how a political leader could have been so cruel.

The rule of Stalin

> **Activity**
>
> It would be very difficult to argue that Stalin's methods of establishing a police state were not effective.
>
> 1 However, for each method you should be able to assess their effectiveness. Complete the table below to help you.
>
> | Method | Summary of what was done | In what ways was it effective? | Mark out of six: 0 = not effective; 6 = very effective | Judgement |
> |---|---|---|---|---|
> | OGPU/NKVD | | | | |
> | Military | | | | |
> | Show trials | | | | |
> | Great Terror | | | | |
> | Gulag camps | | | | |
>
> 2 Now use the information in your chart to write a plan for the following question: Assess the effectiveness of the methods used by Stalin to establish a police state.

How successful were Stalin's agricultural policies in the 1930s?

The success of Stalin's agricultural policies can be judged in terms of three issues:
- economic – the extent to which food production levels were increased as a result of improved productivity
- social – improved living and working conditions for the people of Russia
- political – greater control over the people to ensure the consolidation of communism in Russia.

Before considering these areas, it is important to be clear about how and why Stalin stuck rigidly to the principles of his agricultural policy known as collectivisation.

What was collectivisation?

Context and definitions

Collectivisation refers to the process of bringing a number of small farm units together to form bigger farms. The idea was that peasants would then collaborate to produce much more food to feed both themselves and the growing urban proletariat. Farms would be managed so that land was utilised in the optimum way to ensure that nobody starved. This system was based on the belief that shortages were due mainly to surpluses being hoarded until they could be sold in markets at the highest possible prices. Such a practice was allowed under the NEP but Stalin came to view it as bourgeois and anti-revolutionary.

From the beginning, the Bolsheviks wanted to create collective farms but stalled as a result of resistance from peasants to losing ownership and control over their land. Lenin urged the need for a gradual approach to collectivisation to be taken, which would result in the creation of 'civilised co-operatives' but many considered this unacceptable during a food crisis. Thus, just before Stalin emerged as leader of the USSR, only about 3 per cent of peasant farmers were working on a collective.

Why collectivisation?

The famine of 1927–28 sparked Stalin's desire to push for mass collectivisation. However, this was just a trigger; there were broader motives for wanting to change the way food production was achieved.

- Stalin was motivated by the wish to create 'socialism in the countryside'. In turn, this involved getting rid of the NEP, eradicating the so-called wealthier class of peasants, or *kulaks*, and marginalising 'rightists' who supported a more commercially based agricultural policy. All of these policies and groups were seen as traitors to the revolution and opponents of Stalinist rule.
- Stalin understood, like other Russian leaders before him, that to modernise industry, a revolution in agricultural production also had to occur. Rural workers had to increase their productivity to meet, what would follow under the Five Year Plans, a dramatic increase in demand for food from an expanding urban proletariat.

Type: voluntary or forced?

Stalin's collectivisation policy got underway in November 1929 and went hand in hand with 'the liquidation of the *kulaks* as a class' (see pages 116–17). Stalinists saw this as a 'class war in the countryside' that was to be carried out quickly and systematically. Collectivisation was actually meant to be voluntary but, in reality, it usually occurred as follows.

- The principles of collectivisation were explained to villagers at special meetings organised by **plenipotentiaries**.
- A mixture of poorer peasants, Komsomols and 'politically aware' workers were recruited to seek out wealthier peasants and denounce them as *kulaks*. This helped create a sense of fear within a community, which subsequently made it much easier to encourage others to sign up to the collective programme. Other incentives were offered such as the prospect of working with a new tractor and combine harvester.
- The result was the formation of either **Kolkhozy** ('pure' collectives) or **Sovkhozy** (state collectives).

How far did any benefits of collectivisation outweigh the costs?

Judgement about whether the benefits of collectivisation outweighed the costs can be usefully made by considering the evidence for the economic, social and political outcomes of the policy.

Economic

The main economic indicators to focus on are food production levels and the variables that affected access to food for the bulk of the population, see Table 1.

Table 1 Agricultural statistics, 1922–40

Factor	1922	1929	1930	1931	1932	1933	1934	1935	1940
Grain harvest (million tonnes)	50.3	71.7	83.5	69.5	69.6	68.4	67.6	75.0	77.0
State procurement of grain (million tonnes)		16.1	22.1	22.8	18.5	22.6			
Grain exports (million tonnes)		0.9	4.8	5.1	1.7	1.7			
Cattle (million head)		67.1	52.3	47.9	40.1	38.4	42.4	49.3	
Pigs (million head)		26.0	20.4	13.6	14.4	11.6	12.1	17.4	
Sheep and goats (million head)		147.0	108.8	77.7	52.1	50.2	51.9	61.1	
Eggs (billion)		9.2							9.6
Milk (million tonnes)		29.3							26.5
Mineral fertilisers (million tonnes)		0.1							1.1
Tractors (thousand)		1.3							31.6

Source: Alec Nove, *An Economic History of the U.S.S.R.*, Pelican, 1982, page 186.

The following conclusions can be drawn from Table 1.
- Grain production initially increased dramatically, but then evened off.
- The state procured (took) an amount of grain for redistribution, export or as a safety net against famine but this remained stable.
- Grain exports fell significantly after 1931 suggesting a move towards autarky (self-sufficiency) and concerns about the need to feed an expanding population at home.
- The use of new scientific and technological ideas was minimal although the table gives no indication as to why the take up of science and technology in agriculture was so poor relative to the West.

In general, Table 1 supports the notion that the late 1920s witnessed progress in agriculture but the 1930s were a period of stagnation (although not decline).

Mechanisation

It was hoped that by grouping farms together in collectives it would increase efficiency through the effective use of agricultural machinery. The motorised tractor became the symbol of the new mechanised farming and the regime hoped that this would also result in a decrease in the numbers needed to work on the farms so that they could be used in the new factories. Despite the mechanisation programme, which involved the establishment of motor tractor stations to provide machines for the collectives, these machines often broke down and the lack of trained specialists and mechanics hindered their effectiveness. As a result, increases in output of grain were slow to be seen.

Social

By March 1930, Stalin claimed that 58 per cent of all households had been collectivised, which was a gross exaggeration. Nevertheless, 'mass collectivisation' had a dramatic effect as witnessed by widespread opposition from peasants and local officials. Such resistance often took the form of direct action, as was the case at Bransk Oblast where peasants actually drove away a party of Komsomols who tried to seize the church bells. Resistance came in other forms such as migration. In Kazakhstan, collectivisation virtually destroyed the nomadic way of life. The peasants there reacted by moving out of the region into China. The population of Kazakhstan fell by 75 per cent within a few years.

Stalin blamed this kind of scenario on regional officials whom, he argued, had become 'intoxicated with success'. By the end of March 1930, the pace of collectivisation slackened and Stalin coupled this with a proclamation allowing peasants to quit collectives they had recently signed up to. The inevitable mass exodus followed, only to be quickly clamped down on by renewed pressure to collectivise by the end of the year.

The famine of 1932–34 disrupted the development of collectivisation. A combination of the effects of the first phase of collectivisation and poor harvests due to terrible weather conditions led to the most disastrous famine of the whole period. Although the number of deaths resulting from starvation and disease was similar to that for the 1921 famine, many more suffered as a result of repression by the Stalinist regime.
- The death penalty was imposed for stealing grain (even though the grain might have legally belonged to the accused).
- Peasants who ate their own seed corn were shot along with those sent to guard it.

The social benefits of Collectivisation

There were some benefits for the peasantry. Probably the greatest improvement was that electricity was brought to some villages, allowing the installation of lights in homes. There was also the building of schools, which led to some improvement in literacy rates, and sanitorium, which provided the first health care that many had ever known. Creches were provided for young children and babies, but this was so that the women could go and work on the collectives.

- Discussion of the grain crisis was banned; this was a necessity as Stalin publicly denied a food problem existed.
- Severe restrictions were also placed on those who wanted to move around to look for food.
- The reaction of some peasants did not seem to help. Animals were slaughtered in preference to handing them over to the authorities. A horse shortage ensued which slowed down the ploughing of fields. Cattle often froze to death on collectives that lacked big enough barns to house them.

By 1935, matters seemed to improve and food production increased slowly. However, on the eve of the Second World War it was unlikely that total food output had reached pre-First World War levels. Generally, the diet of workers in particular seemed to worsen under the communists. By the late 1930s, for example, the consumption of meat and fish had fallen by 80 per cent.

Partly as a result of the famine, a special charter was issued in 1935 to improve payments to farmers in the *Kolkhozy* and to give owners of small plots more legal security. Interestingly, but not surprisingly, the small plots proved more productive than the collective farms especially when it came to supplying dairy goods.

The move back towards intensive collectivisation resulted in about 50 per cent of all peasants once again being brought together in *Kolkhozy*. By the end of 1937, the figure had increased to 93 per cent. In contrast to the first wave of collectives, peasants were now allowed to keep small plots of land. Also, blocks of 40 farms were organised through motor tractor stations. As the title suggests, these were originally organisations through which tractors and other heavy equipment could be loaned to peasants. The motor tractor station became responsible for distributing seed, collecting grain, establishing levels of payment for produce and deciding on what produce farmers could keep for their own consumption.

By 1941, 98 per cent of all peasant households worked on collectives. Despite an improvement in conditions on collective farms they were still disliked by peasants.

There were a number of reasons for resistance.
- The traditional way of organising farming was valued by peasants. The abolition of the **mir** in 1930 was considered a major blow to village autonomy.
- Collectives deprived peasants of the right to make extra income, which would keep them just above subsistence level. It also placed restrictions on the variety of crops that could be grown and other rural activities that had previously been tolerated and enjoyed.
- The 1932–34 famine suggested that many that collectives were likely to contribute to food shortages rather than relieve them. Many believed that as requisitioning was part of the collectivisation policy the famine was largely 'man made'.

Political

Under Stalin, collectivisation went hand-in-hand with dekulakisation. The treatment of *kulaks* during this period followed a similar pattern throughout Russia. Wealthier peasants were 'visited' by Komsomols and plenipotentiaries. *Kulak* houses would then be stripped bare in an attempt to locate hidden wealth. Clothing, food, fuel, furniture and other personal belongings were confiscated and sold or given away to other villagers. In anticipation, *kulaks* often sold their goods, slaughtered animals and even abandoned their homes to flee to the towns. If caught by the authorities, their fate depended on how they were categorised.

- 'Fortunate' *kulaks* were those who were reallocated land often of a very poor quality. They were then given unrealistic food production targets, which they invariably failed to meet. The result was that they were deported to Gulag work camps in inhospitable places such as Siberia.
- Standard *kulaks* were simply robbed and sent straight to Gulag camps where they tended to die fairly quickly.
- Malicious, ideological or 'sub'-*kulaks* (*zlostnye*) were those who actively opposed collectivisation. They either were transported immediately, again to Gulags, or were more likely to be shot.

It is estimated that from the beginning of 1928 to the end of 1930, between 1 million and 3 million *kulak* families (6–18 million people) were deported and about 30,000 *kulaks* were shot. In this sense Stalin achieved his aim to 'liquidate the *kulaks*' as a class. However, in many ways *kulaks* were a myth. The term was invented to provide an excuse to blame certain people for the failings of communist agricultural policies. Up to the end of the period there were always some peasant farmers who seemed to be more productive than others, simply because they were good at farming. To classify them as an elite group within the peasant class was a deliberate exaggeration.

Although most historians have condemned the policy as both brutal and ineffective it should not be forgotten that for the first time the establishment of collective farms did give the Party control of the Russian peasantry, which had not been possible when there were lots of small farms.

Activity

The key focus on the issue of collectivisation is likely to be on the extent to which it can be considered a success. Much will depend upon the criteria you use, whether it is production levels or the social and human cost.

1. How valid is the view that collectivisation was a success? Use the following table to help you answer the question.

Evidence that collectivisation was a success	Evidence that collectivisation was a failure

2. You might find it helpful to use a range of colours to identify the following issues in the table:
   - economic
   - social
   - political
   - human.

3. In light of the evidence in your table, what is your view? Write a paragraph to explain your view and support it with evidence from the table. Are there some areas where there was more success than failure?

How successful were Stalin's industrial policies in the late 1920s and 1930s?

The successes of Stalin's industrial policies can be measured by considering how far he met his aims for industry using centralised planning.

The first two Five Year Plans: aims and effects

Aims

There were two general aims that underpinned Stalinist economic policy.

1 One was to launch a war against Russia's tsarist past. Stalin believed that Russia had failed to keep up with the West due to the incompetence of the tsarist regimes but more generally because the tsars were enemies of the workers. Only with a system that allowed more worker autonomy and that encouraged workers to believe that they were the key to economic success, would Russia become a major industrial force.

2 The second aim was to prepare for potential conflict with Russia's capitalist enemies. The development of heavy industry was the key to expansion and modernisation of the armed forces, which was essential to the defence of Russia. These aims were also linked to the wish for **economic autarky.**

Stalin believed that the only way his aims could be achieved was by abandoning the NEP completely and replacing it with a policy based on strict state control and centralised planning. Industrialisation was to be stimulated through the setting of production targets. These targets were to be achieved over a series of five-year periods. From 1929 to 1964, there were seven Five Year Plans. Ironically, this policy involved very little strategic planning in the modern sense. Targets were set by the ruling elite and were often based on very flimsy research. Managers at local level were ordered to achieve them and were in constant fear of failing.

In theory, there was a structure to the target setting and planning process. It resembled the following.

- Initial targets were stipulated by key officials in the party. **Gosplan** (the State Planning Commission) was given the task of researching and calculating figures needed for target setting for individual industries.
- Targets and other appropriate information were then passed on to industrial commissariats (official departments) to frame a plan of some sort for clearly defined areas of economic activity. Initially, there were four commissariats (heavy industry, which was the most important, light industry, timber and food). By the beginning of the third Five Year Plan, there were twenty of these bodies.
- The 'plans' were then passed on to regional managers/directors to implement. In reality, the plans were little more than very detailed instructions about what had to be achieved. There was very little guidance on how targets were to be arrived at and on the availability of resources needed to support the planning process.

Economic effects

The first plan was officially introduced in the spring of 1929 at the Sixteenth Party Congress. As it was outlined then, it covered the period from October 1928 to September 1933. In practice, the first plan, as with the second, did not run its full course, coming to an end in December 1932. This was owing to the government exaggerating its achievements, claiming that the plans were so successful that targets had been met well ahead of schedule. The reality was that workers had struggled to meet what were totally unrealistic targets especially after Stalin audaciously decided to revise them upwards towards the end of each plan. Nevertheless, centralised planning was the main characteristic of industrialisation until the end of the period.

A summary of what was achieved can be seen in Table 2 below.

Table 2 Achievements of the Five Year Plans, 1928–45

Product	1928	1940	1945
Electricity (million kilowatt-hours)	5.0	48.3	43.3
Oil (million tonnes)	11.6	31.1	19.4
Coal (million tonnes)	35.5	166	150
Gas (million cubic metres)	0.3	3.4	3.4
Steel (million tonnes)	4.3	18.3	12.3
Tractors (thousands)	1.3	31.6	7.7
Plastics and synthetics (thousand tonnes)	–	10.9	21.3
Clocks and watches (millions)	0.9	2.8	0.3
Cement (million tonnes)	1.8	5.7	1.8

Source: J.N. Westwood, *Endurance and Endeavour: Russian History 1812–2001*, Oxford University Press, 2002, page 614.

The statistics in Table 2 need to be treated with caution. They are based partly on 'official records' but also on adjustments made by historians to compensate for inaccuracy. Under the first two plans, managers quite obviously submitted false claims about production levels, as they feared the possible consequences of not achieving the set targets. Fabrication of production levels backfired on the managers when Stalin became so impressed with achievement that he revised the targets. However, it is understandable why managers did this given the climate of fear that had been manufactured and what would happen to them if they failed to meet the targets. Nevertheless, the statistical 'evidence' suggests that each plan had some success.

It should also be remembered that half the machine tools being used in Russia by 1932 had been installed since 1928. For the first time the Urals and the area beyond it was being exploited economically and it resulted in the development of new industrial towns, with the most famous being Magnitogorsk with its iron-works and blast furnaces.

The first two plans had successes as well as limitations, as outlined in Table 3.

Table 3 Successes and limitations of the Five Year Plans, 1928–65

Plan	Successes	Limitations
1: October 1928–December 1932	There were significant increases in the output of heavy industry. The engineering industry developed considerably especially with respect to the production of machine tools and turbines. New specialised industrial centres emerged, for example, Magnitogorsk in the Urals. Agriculture was stimulated as tractor works expanded.	**Consumer industries** were neglected causing discontent among certain sectors of society. Small specialist workshops disappeared. A shortage of skilled workers was apparent. This was partly because of show trials and purges. Although production levels rose, targets were not met. There was quite a dramatic shortfall in some industries, such as chemicals.
2: January 1933–December 1937	The electricity industry took off and heavy industry built on the base laid by the first plan. Over 4500 new enterprises were started. Engineering became self-sufficient and no longer relied on imports of specialist equipment. Something resembling a genuine transport and communications network was put in place. The chemical industry made up for the lack of progress during the first plan. Certain metals were mined for the first time – tin, zinc and copper. Specialised training schemes for workers were implemented. Targets were scaled down and a more rational approach to planning was adopted. The commissariats were better organised and more effective.	Consumer industries continued to decline although some flourished, for example, footwear, meat packaging, ice-cream. The oil industry was very slow to expand compared with Western counterparts.
3: January 1938–June 1941	Production and productivity in heavy industry continued to be impressive although regional variations became more apparent. There was a notable improvement in the quantity and quality of armaments produced.	Russia's entry into the Great Patriotic War (1941) led to a diversion of resources to fuel the war effort. There was a shortage of raw materials. There was generally a slowdown in the pace of progress. Some historians have attributed this to the purges as well as the war. By the end of the third Five Year Plan there were many features of a lack of planning: shortages, bottlenecks and a lack of 'expert' workers.

Social effects

The impact of economic policies is highly debatable. One interpretation is that they led to more regular employment and therefore more stable incomes for families. This gave the Russian people greater access to better housing, healthcare, consumer items and education. As the state became the main provider of work, it naturally also became the provider of all the social institutions and facilities that were associated with the need for a fit and healthy workforce. In order to bring about increased industrial production a more educated workforce was required and many benefited from increased educational opportunities with some 200,000 in higher education and nearly 1 million in secondary technical schools.

Another view is that this needs to be balanced against the lack of choice of material goods that existed but, more importantly, the restrictions that were placed on individuals and groups who did not toe the Party line.

It is clear that a more equitable society came at the cost of a reduction in personal freedoms as any vestiges of worker's rights disappeared as free trade unions were abolished and a code of 'labour discipline' was imposed, which introduced a range of punishments from loss of wages to imprisonment in labour camps. In order to achieve the targets worker's interests and living conditions were of little interest to the regime with most living in overcrowded tenements, often with four or five families sharing a toilet and kitchen. The regime may have claimed that wages improved, but as there was food rationing and higher prices living standards were actually lower in 1937 than they had been in 1928.

Political effects

The main political effect of Stalinist economic policies was that centralised planning of the economy went hand in hand with a centralised, rather than devolved, political system. Very little political power was filtered down to regional level. Also, economic reforms were used to control opposition. Any individual or group that showed any hint of sabotaging economic planning and/or collectivisation were severely dealt with.

Although it is easier to make out a case for the success of the Five Year Plans than collectivisation, some argue that even this does not justify the human cost and suffering. However, some have argued that the harsh measures were needed given the economic problems the country faced. Most importantly, this has led historians, such as Peter Gattrell, to argue that it was these policies that allowed Russia to survive the **Great Patriotic War** from 1941–5 and emerge as a superpower in the post-war period.

Activity

1. Consider the following statements and find evidence from this section and further research to either support or challenge the statements.
   - The Five Year Plans were not well planned.
   - The Five Year Plans transformed the Russian economy and enabled it to defeat Germany.
   - The Five Year Plans brought more benefits than losses to the workers.
   - Worker's conditions deteriorated considerably under the Five Year Plans.
   - The plans were largely a failure, but officials and managers were too frightened to acknowledge the problems.
   - The plans succeeded in kick-starting the Russian economy.
2. Which of the statements do you most agree with? Explain your choice.

Historical debate

Was Stalin the natural heir of Lenin?

A major area of debate among historians is the extent to which the Stalinist state was the creation of Lenin. Some have argued that Stalin was the natural heir of Lenin, while others have argued that there was a break between the two regimes and have suggested that Stalin changed the course of Russian history. Those who have argued that he was the natural heir of Lenin have seen Stalin's regime as an extension of the authoritarian and centralised rule of the earlier regime. However, those who argue that there was a break point to changes made to virtually all institutions of government and to the totalitarian nature of the Stalinist regime.

Russia 1894–1941

Activity

1. Summarise the views of the two passages. Which of the views do you find more convincing? Explain your choice.
2. Using this section and further research, what evidence is there to support the views that:
   - Stalin's dictatorship was a logical extension of Lenin's authoritarian and centralised regime
   - Stalin exercised personal control and used terror to a degree that would have been unimaginable under Lenin
   - institutionally and ideologically, Lenin laid the foundations for Stalin, but the passage from Leninism to the worse horrors of Stalinism was not smooth and inevitable.

Read these two passages that offer different views of Stalinism:

Passage 1

Stalin sincerely regarded himself as a disciple of Lenin, a man destined to carry out his agenda to a successful conclusion. With one exception, the killing of fellow Communists – a crime Lenin did not commit – he faithfully implemented Lenin's domestic and foreign programmes. He prevented the party from being riven by factionalism; he liquidated the 'noxious' intelligentsia; he collectivised agriculture, as Lenin had desired; he subjected the Russian economy to a single plan; he industrialised Russia; he built a powerful red Army and he helped unleash the Second World War, which had been one of Lenin's objectives as well.

R. Pipes, *Three Whys of the Russian Revolution*, Pimlico, 1998

Passage 2

What is important is that these events were not the natural flow-on of earlier developments; they were sharp breaks resulting from conscious decisions by leading political actors. This means that arguments that see Stalinism as the inevitable product of the 1917 revolution or of Leninism/Bolshevism as mistaken. Both the revolution and the corpus of theory which the Bolsheviks carried with them had elements which were consistent with the Soviet phenomenon, just as they had elements that were totally inconsistent with it. However, it needed the direct intervention on the part of the political actors in introducing the revolution from above and the terror to realise the Stalinist phenomenon in Soviet society.

G. Gill, *Stalinism*, Palgrave, 1990

Further research

Edward Acton and Tom Stableford, *The Soviet Union: A Documentary History, Volume 1, 1917–1940*, University of Exeter Press, 2005

Edward Acton and Tom Stableford, *The Soviet Union: A Documentary History, Volume 2, 1939–1991*, University of Exeter Press, 2007.

Anne Applebaum, *Gulag: A History of Soviet Camps*, Penguin, 2003

Robert Conquest, *The Great Terror: A Reassessment*, Oxford University Press, 1990

Orlando Figes, *The Whisperers: Private Life in Stalin's Russia*, Penguin, 2007

Sheila Fitzpatrick, *Everyday Stalinism: Ordinary Life in Extraordinary Times: Soviet Russia in the 1930s*, Oxford University Press, 1999

Catriona Kelly, *Comrade Pavlik: The Rise and Fall of a Soviet Boy Hero*, Granta Books, 2005

Christopher Read (ed.), *The Stalin Years. A Reader*, Palgrave Macmillan, 2005

Simon Sebag Montefiore, *Stalin: The Court of the Red Tsar*, Phoenix, 2004

Robert Service, *A History of Modern Russia: From Nicholas II to Putin*, Penguin, 2003

Aleksandr Solzhenitsyn, *One Day in the Life of Ivan Denisovich*, Penguin, 2000

John Steinbeck, *A Russian Journal*, Penguin, 2000

Chapter takeaways

- Stalin was a complex character. He was ruthless, but also feared that others were always out to get him and topple him from power. As a leader, he showed the ability to manoeuvre others into positions of weakness but also to get them to agree to his viewpoint. The latter was done through a mixture of repression and reform.
- Divisions within the Bolshevik party came to the fore after Lenin's death in 1924. The divisions led to a power struggle between Stalin, Trotsky, Kamenev and Zinoviev. Through cunning and manipulation Stalin triumphed and eventually had his main rivals killed.
- After gaining power Stalin strengthened his position through the astute use of propaganda to create a cult of personality. Censorship also helped him consolidate power as it limited the possibility of opposing views being heard.
- To complement the use of propaganda and censorship, Stalin deployed force through the secret police. The latter instilled fear in the people and was integral to creating the Great Terror of the mid-1930s.
- Stalin used economic and social reforms to control the behaviour of Russian people, but also to improve Russia's world standing. Collectivisation and further industrialisation through the Five Year Plans resulted in the greater production of goods and services so that Russia could become mostly self-sufficient.
- By 1941, Russia was in a relatively strong position to stave off external threats, especially from Germany. However, the over reliance on Stalin led to disasters in 1941 and it was only in the longer term that the industrial developments of the 1930s, and the rigid and uncompromising party discipline enabled the USSR to recover from the heavy losses of 1941 and finally defeat Nazi Germany.

Study skills: Writing a conclusion and overall essay writing

The types of question set for AS and A Level essays will be the same and therefore all the advice in this section applies to both examinations.

Writing a conclusion

What is the purpose of a conclusion? A conclusion should come to a judgement that is based on what you have already written and should be briefly supported. It should not introduce new ideas – if they were important they should have been discussed in the main body of the essay. You must also take care to avoid offering a contrary argument to the one you have pursued throughout the rest of the essay as that will suggest that you have not thought through your ideas and are unclear as to what you think.

It might be that you are largely re-stating the view you offered in the vital opening paragraph, or in stronger answers there might be a subtle variation to the judgement – you confirm your original view, but suggest, with an example, that there were occasions when this was not always correct.

If the question has named a factor then you should give a judgement about that factor's relative importance, either explaining why it is or is not the most important, and the role it played in the events you have discussed. If the question asks you to assess a range of factors, the conclusion should explain which you think is the most important and should support the claim. At first sight a claim might appear to be judgement, but without supporting material it is no more than an assertion and will not gain credit.

Russia 1894–1941

Consider the essay question in the Example box:

Example

'Stalin's leadership and political skills were the most important reason why he was able to consolidate his power.' How far do you agree?

In order to answer this question you may consider:

- Stalin's experience as general secretary of the Communist party
- the use of repression and reform
- Stalin's personality.

Now consider this sample conclusion, written in response to the question in the Example box:

Sample answer

To conclude, there is evidence to support the view that, especially in the early stages of his rule, Stalin was able to use his experience and skill as General Secretary of the party to control and eliminate challengers to his position. Unless he had won the core of party membership over to support him, he would not have been able to further consolidate his power through the use of repression and reform. It is possible that, especially when Stalin's repressive measures are focused upon, he may be seen as consolidating power as a result of purely a psychotic and paranoid personality. However, this would ignore the fact that he showed the requisite leadership qualities and political skills to get him into a position of power and to maintain it until his death.

This is a good final paragraph because:
- it focuses immediately on the issue in the question
- it provides a clear judgement on that issue
- that judgement is supported with good argument and evidence
- it briefly summarises what the writer believes was the main reason.

Question practice

In light of these comments and the sample conclusion, write conclusions to the following questions.
1. 'Divisions in the Bolshevik party from 1917 to 1929 were the result of ideological differences.' How far do you agree?
2. How important was the cult of personality in enabling Stalin to consolidate power?
3. To what extent was dekulakisation the result of Stalin's need to explain the failings of collectivisation?

Short answer essay question

Which of the following contributed more to the economic development of the Soviet Union before 1941?
(i) Collectivisation
(ii) Five-Year Plans

Explain your answer with reference to both (i) and (ii).

You have now covered all the main skills you need to write a good essay. It is worth looking back at these skills before you write each essay you are set. This will help you to build up and reinforce the skills you need for the examination and ensure that you are familiar with the skills needed to do well.

Russia 1894–1941

Revision for the non-British Period Studies essay

It is important, and will be more productive, if you make your revision active rather than simply try to learn large amounts of factual material about Russia in the period from 1894 to 1941. In revising the material you may have had **wider experience of historical study and further developed the skills** that you need for this element of the paper:

- focusing on the issue in the question
- analysing the issues
- evaluating the relative importance of the issues and factors
- reaching supported judgements about the issue in the question.

Having studied all four key topics (split into four chapters in this book), you will also be able to see the whole period in its broader context, rather than seeing each key topic in isolation. **In light of this, you should review** some of the judgements you made about the issues and questions raised in the earlier topics.

It might be a **good starting point** to consider the key questions at the start of each chapter. When you first studied the chapter you may have noted down your view of each question, it would be **valuable to go and revisit** that view and decide in light of further study whether you want to change it. It would be a good idea to plan an essay answer to each key question. This will not only ensure that you have sufficient material available when you reach the examination room, but also ensure you have thought about issues around which examination questions are likely to be set.

Remember when planning answers:

- What is your overall view about the question?
- What issues do you need to cover?
- What would be your opening sentences for each paragraph?
- What evidence would you use to support or challenge the idea you have raised in each sentence?

A **planning sheet**, such as the one on the following page might provide a structure.

Essay title	
View about question:	
Key ideas:	

Opening sentence	Evidence to support	Evidence to challenge
Judgement:		

You may also have written essays on some of the key questions. **Re-read the essays**.
- Do you still agree with the view you put forward?
- Is the essay balanced? Does it consider both sides of the argument?
- Is the judgement developed?
- How would you improve the essay?

In light of this, you could produce a new plan or, using the advice in the Study skills sections of this book, write a new conclusion that develops the judgement.

The Study skills section in each chapter of this book also contains examples of possible essay questions. You could produce plans for those questions, or write opening or concluding paragraphs for them.

As you can see, all of the suggestions involve you being active and not simply reading through and trying to learn your notes. This approach will help to keep you focused and help to ensure that you have thought about the issues that are likely to be raised in examination questions.

Answering AS interpretation questions

The OCR specification H505 states the two (of four) key topics from which the interpretation question will be set. They have been specifically chosen because there are areas of debate among historians and are about issues that you will have considered in the classroom. The interpretation will be from a named historian, but you do not need to comment about the writer, in fact it does not matter if you have not heard of them – what matters is what their view of an event or issue is. The interpretation will be no more than a few sentences long, but there will be enough for you to understand what the writer is saying about the issue. The question will always be phrased in the same way and ask you to evaluate the strengths and limitations of the interpretation, as can be seen in the example below.

> **Example**
>
> Despite efforts at political reform, urban Russia on the brink of the First World War arguably found itself on the brink of a new revolution.
> Orlando Figes, *Revolutionary Russia 1891–1991*, 2004
>
> **Evaluate the strengths and limitations of this interpretation, making reference to other interpretations that you have studied.**

Opening paragraph: placing the interpretation in the context of the debate

The mark scheme requires you to have a thorough understanding of the wider historical debate from which the interpretation is taken if you are to reach the higher levels. It might be helpful to start your answer by explaining what the interpretation is saying; in this example that would be that a revolution was likely in towns and cities in Russia in 1914. You would then go on to place the Interpretation in the context of the debate about the extent to which Russia was stable on the eve of the war and be able to explain some of the different views that have been offered. Having explained the Interpretation you could then go on to explain that this view has been challenged by those who have argued that Russia was stable and that it was the war that caused revolution. However, whatever you do, you must NOT evaluate these other interpretations, you are simply placing the interpretation you have been given in the wider context of the debate.

So to recap, the opening paragraph of your answer to an interpretation question should:
- explain the given interpretation
- place the given interpretation in the context of the wider debate from which it is drawn.

Structuring your answer

The main focus of your answer should be to evaluate the strengths and limitations of the given interpretation, which should be done by applying your own knowledge to the interpretation. It will be helpful to remember what is meant by the term 'evaluation' – you are giving a value to the interpretation. Is it convincing or not? What knowledge do you have that either supports or challenges this interpretation? You may know a great deal about the debate, but it is important that you use this knowledge and link it to the actual interpretation given and do not simply write all you know about the debate with no link to the interpretation as this would simply turn your answer into another period study essay. It might, therefore, be helpful to build up a working vocabulary of evaluative words and phrases. These might include simple words such as valid or invalid, however, indeed, furthermore and moreover, but it might also include phrases such as 'this is given further credibility by' or 'this view is challenged by'.

If we go back to the interpretation from Orlando Figes, we can begin to apply knowledge to it and link that knowledge to the interpretation.

> **Sample answer**
>
> This view is *given credence* by the failure of attempts at political reform, since the *duma* became a mere talking shop, with members pleading with the Tsar to give them more control over their own affairs. Tensions reached a head in the summer of 1914 when a *general strike* was called, which members of the *duma* openly supported. The interpretation correctly acknowledges there were efforts at political reform, but that these were heavily controlled by the tsar's own advisers, to the extent that election results were doctored.

You can go through this example and see the knowledge that is used and how it is linked to the interpretation. You should also see that the depth of knowledge used is no greater than that you would use in a period study essay.

This paragraph has considered some of the strengths of the interpretation and you may develop this further before, in the next paragraph looking at the limitations. The approach will be exactly the same, linking your knowledge that challenges the interpretation to it and not simply writing an essay. It might start with something like this:

> **Sample answer**
>
> However, this interpretation misses the point about the fundamental stability of the Tsarist regime in 1914, and its resilience in the face of adversity. Most importantly, the troops remained loyal to the Tsar and the revolutionary groups were either still in exile or on the fringe of the political scene. This meant that the cities were relatively safe, and despite the violence of 1914, the revolutionary threat did not really exist. The interpretation also ignores the improved economic outlook in the urban centres in 1914, and the lack of real efforts at political reform. Economic growth in the years to 1914 was six percent per year, and Russia became a major textile manufacturer. Political reform beyond the creation of the *dumas* did not exist, and the October Manifesto had not weakened the authority of the Tsar at all.

So to recap, your answer to an interpretation question should:
- contain a paragraph on the strengths of the interpretation
- followed by a paragraph on the limitations of the interpretation
- show your detailed knowledge of the debate
- link the knowledge to the interpretation using evaluative words and phrases.

The provenance of the interpretation and other areas to avoid

You might be surprised to discover that you do not need to know anything about the historian. There is a good chance that you may never have heard of the writer; do not worry, you are evaluating using your knowledge of the debate. This means you should not consider the provenance of the interpretation, that is, who wrote it, when it was written or the tone of the writing. Remember, this is not a primary source and it is very unlikely that who wrote it or when it was written will impact on the validity of the view offered.

You should also avoid the historiographical approach, either where you describe or evaluate other historians' views. The focus, once you have placed the interpretation in context, should be on the interpretation you have been given. Do not write about the various schools of history. For this topic, you might be tempted to write about orthodox or revisionist views, but again this should be avoided as it does not matter what 'school' the writer is from – you may not be able to tell from the short piece you are given anyway – simply evaluate what you have been given!

Now try this on these following examples.

Examples

Evaluate the strengths and limitations of this interpretation, making reference to other interpretations that you have studied.

1. The question of whether Russia would have become a modern industrial state but for the war and the revolution is in essence a meaningless one. One may say that statistically the answer is in the affirmative.

    A. Nove, *An Economic History of the USSR*, 1973

2. Despite everything, traditions of loyalty to Tsarism survived among many sections of the population. These resurfaced immediately after the declaration of war. In the duma criticism of the government ceased. So did the demonstrations and strikes in the capital.

    D. Christian, *Imperial and Soviet Russia*, 1997

3. He [Lenin] was not a democrat; he did not deal in compromise. He was a revolutionary who believed that the only way to govern was not by compromise but by crushing the opposition. Hence his response to the Constituent Assembly.

    M. Lynch, *Russia 1894–1941*, 2015

4. The civil war permanently marked Soviet society. It completed the work, begun by the revolution, of destroying the old society. The institutions of the new society could be created anew by any force which could control it. That force was the Communist party.

    G. Hosking, *Russia and the Russians*, 2001

5. If the seeds of dictatorship lay in ideology, they only came fruition in the face of remorseless demands placed on party and state by civil war and economic collapse.

    S. Smith, *The Russian Revolution*, 2002

Glossary

Amazons Generally female warriors, specifically in this context the First Petrograd Women's Battalion.

Attritional warfare A type of warfare whereby two sides attempt to wear down each other's resources through sustained bombardments and troop attacks.

Bolsheviks A term, coined by Lenin, denoting 'majority' (taken from the Russian *bolshinstvo*); Lenin used this name to give the impression that he and his supporters were in the majority in 1903.

Blockade The use of naval forces to prevent ships entering or leaving ports.

Civil war A war between different groups within a country.

Comintern The Communist International, a body set up in Moscow in March 1919 to organise worldwide revolution.

Constitutional monarchy A system of government in which the monarch rules but governs through elected representatives whose decisions cannot be countermanded.

Consumer industries These included any industries producing goods and services for direct consumption by the population, for example, those producing clothing, ovens, cooking utensils, toys for children.

Division of labour The allocation of particular, often specialist, tasks to individual workers who are organised into a production line.

Dogma A solid set of principles or beliefs.

Duma The Russian parliament that existed from 1906 to 1917.

Eastern Front The Eastern Front was where the German and Austrian-Hungarian forces met the Russian forces in Eastern Europe.

Economic autarky When a country can provide all of the resources it needs without having to trade.

Emancipation of the serfs An announcement, in 1861, that peasants would be freed from being owned, like any other property, by wealthy landowners and the state.

Factionalist One who went about pursuing his or her own interests to the detriment of party unity. Factionalism involved forming opposition groups within government and party.

Franchise The right to vote.

Gold standard This involved the fixing of a country's currency to a specific quantity (and therefore value) of gold.

Gosplan A body originally set up in 1921 to plan for industrialisation and economic growth.

Great Patriotic War The term used in Russia to describe the period of the Second World War in which the Soviet Union was defending the country following the German invasion in 1941.

Gross national product (GNP) A measurement of an economy's level of wealth and therefore living standards: the total value of all the final products and services produced by the means of production owned by a country's residents, includes value earned abroad.

Gulag The organisation that organised the labour camps that were used to house political dissidents and those suspected of being anti-communist, camps often informally refer to as gulags after the organisation that ran them.

In kind This was the payment other than by using money, such as the exchange of goods and services.

Justices of the peace Landowners appointed as officials to maintain law and order at a local level. They worked in conjunction with the police.

Kolkhozy A farm owned and partly organised by the state but worked on by peasant farmers not directly employed by the state. Members could own a house, a small plot of land and a few animals.

Labour Code Rules for the deployment and control of labour.

Labourist Party They were specifically interested in improving the working conditions of the proletariat.

Land captains Landowners who were appointed, from 1899 onwards, mainly to supervise the work of the regional councils (*Zemstva*) that had been introduced by Alexander II.

Leading cadres These were the 'top' members of the Communist Party responsible for organising and educating the masses.

Lenin Enrolment A campaign aimed to encourage peasants to join the Bolshevik Party.

Lenin's Testament Were notes written by Lenin during December 1922 that expressed his wishes for how the governance of Russia should proceed after his death.

Mensheviks A term denoting 'minority' (taken from the Russian *menshinstvo*); in 1903 Martov led the Menshevik group and ironically he had as much if not more support than Lenin.

Militarisation of labour Workers were forced to work either as labourers or soldiers.

Minister of the interior The senior official responsible for domestic security and stability.

Mir A group of village elders who were responsible for governing the behaviour of members of rural communities or villages.

Nationalised This involved the state control of industry and commerce by taking ownership of the means of production, distribution and exchange of goods and services.

Nomenklatura Officially approved officers, administrators and managers in the communist regime who possessed specialist skills.

Plenipotentiaries These were party officials who had 'total' power at a local level.

Pogrom (also known as 'little thunder') The organised violence (murder and the looting and burning of property) against Jews especially those in the Pale of Settlement.

Polish question The question as to whether the Poles would be allowed self-rule.

Productivity The output per unit of production (a unit usually being a worker and/or machine). Thus, productivity is a useful way of measuring the rate of production (rather than just the total amount produced) and, hence, the efficiency of workers.

Glossary

Proletariat Those who worked in industry and lived in urban areas.

Rabkrin The Workers' and Peasants' Inspectorate, a highly bureaucratic and overstaffed organisation.

Rampant inflation The uncontrollable and rapid increase in the prices of goods and services.

Repartition The re-division of land to give peasants a better share of the more fertile cultivatable area.

Schlieffen Plan The plan put together in 1905 by the Chief of the German General Staff, General Count Alfred Von Schlieffen (1833–1913), to act partly as a blueprint for a German attack in the West.

Slavophiles Those who believed that Western values were corrupting and argued that the Russian nation should promote its own culture, and traditions that could be traced back to the original Slavs or Rus peoples.

Sovkhozy Farms owned by the state and worked on by state employees.

Transcaucasia Region encompassing modern day Armenia, Azerbaijan and Georgia.

Vyborg Manifesto A set of demands from militant *Duma* MPs asking the people of Finland not to pay taxes or serve in the armed forces until the *Duma* was restored.

Westernisers Those who wanted to modernise Russia using Western Europe as a model.

World revolution The idea that communism would not be confined to the Soviet Union but would be spread throughout the world.

Index

A
abdication, Nicolas II 48, 53–6, 66
Acton, E. 40
Adeyenko, A. 107
agriculture 114
   Department of 15
   Stalin's policies 113–17
   see also Five Year Plans
Alexander II 15
Alexander III 16, 26
Alexandra, Tsarina 48, 51–2, 53
All Russian Union of Peasants 32–3
American Relief Association 86, 89
anti-Semitism 24–5
arts, manipulation of 108–9
   see also censorship
attritional warfare 48
Austria, First World War 46–8
autocracy, and Nicolas II 13, 15

B
Badcock, S. 21
Baltic Provinces 24
Battle of Yalu River 29
Battleship Potemkin 32, 108
Beria, L. 110
Bloody Sunday (1905) 30–2, 54
Bobrikov, N. 24
Bogolepov, N. 30
Bolshevik Party 12, 20–1, 33, 54–5, 59–60, 62–5, 74–5
   and civil war 79–85
   and communism 92–5
   divisions in 102–3
   Kronstadt rising 87
   power consolidation 75–8
   power struggle 103
bourgeoisie 89, 111
Brusilov Offensive 47–9
Brusilov, A. 48, 50
Bukharin, N. 103, 105
Bund 24–5

C
Caucasus Region 24, 47, 61
censorship 106–9
census (1897) 17, 22
Central Workers Group 54
Cheka 79, 82, 86, 87, 109
Chernov, V.M. 19, 20, 74
cholera 17, 39
Christianity 24–5
civil society 15
civil war (1918-21)
   causes of 79–80
   chronology 80–5
   consequences 86–8
   end of 85

collectivisation 102, 113–17
Comintern 88, 103
communism 92–3
   introduction of 54
   propaganda 106–9
   see also political system
Communist Party of the Soviet Union (CPSU) 107
Congress of Soviets 75–7
Constituent Assembly 63, 73, 74–5
constitutional changes 93
Constitutional Democratic Party 19
constitutional monarchy 56
Cossacks 79
Council of Labour and Defence 78
Council of Ministers 12
Council of Peoples Commissars 76
Course of Civil Law, A 25
court-martials 35, 37
Crimean War (1853-56) 15, 29
currency 26
   see also economy
Czech Legion 82

D
'dark masses' 17
Dashnaks 24
death penalty 37
   see also executions
Decree on Land 78
Decree on Peace 77
Decree on the Rights of the People of Russia 77–8
Decree on Workers Control 78
democracy 73–5
   see also Constituent Assembly
democratic centralism 92
Denikin, A. 83
Department of Agriculture 15
diktat 47
direct action 19
disease, spread of 17
Dumas
   first 19, 23, 31–5
   fourth (final) 36, 52, 55–6
   'Progressive Bloc' 52, 53
   second 35
   third 35
Dzerzhinsky, F. 86, 87

E
East Prussia 47
Eastern Front 46
economy
   challenges to 16
   collectivisation 114–15
   currency 26
   economic growth 16

   economic policy 26–7
   effect of civil war 88
   foreign investment 16, 26–7
   gross national product (GNP) 38
   impact of First World War 49–50
   inflation 39, 49, 88
   nationalisation 78
   New Economic Policy (NEP) 88–91
   Supreme Economic Council (SEC) 78
eight principles 58
Eisenstein, S. 108
Ekaterinburg 82–3
elections, Constituent Assembly 74
Emancipation Edict (1861) 17, 87
emancipation of the serfs 15
Estonia 62
execution, of royal family 82–3
exportation 16

F
famine 16, 86, 89, 113, 115
Ferdinand, F. 46
Figes, O. 51
film industry 108
Finland 24, 61
First World War
   allies 57
   attritional warfare 48
   Brusilov offensive 47–9
   casualties 47
   consequences of 80
   Eastern Front 46–7
   financial burden 49–50
   Great Retreat 48
   impact of 46–50
   military defeats 47–8
   peace 58, 77
   Russian stability before 39–40
   Schlieffen Plan 46
   withdrawal from 48
Five Year Plans 105–7, 114, 118–21
food supply
   collectivisation 114–15
   exceeding demand 90
   shortages 49–50, 80, 89, 115–16
   see also famine
foreign investment 16, 26–7
free enterprise, lack of 16
freemasons 56
Fundamental Laws 12, 13, 34–5

G
Gapon, G. 31–2
Georgia 24, 62, 80
Georgian Affair 103
Germany 24
Gill, G. 122
Gold Standard 26

Index

Golitsyn, N. 51
Gorky, M. 75
Grand Duke Michael 54
'Great Spurt' 26
Great Terror 101, 110–12
Green armies 80, 85–6
gross national product (GNP) 38
Guchkov, A. 19, 52, 56
Gulag camps 110, 111–12

H
Hitler 65
Hobsbawm, E. 95
Holy Synod 25–6
housing 17, 40
   see also living conditions
Hungary, First World War 46–8

I
industrialisation 15–17, 23, 26–7
industry 89–90
   Stalin's policies 118–21
inflation 39, 49, 88
intelligentsia 19, 30
International Women's Day 54
Izvestiya 63, 107

J
Japan
   Russo-Japanese War 26, 27–30
   Jews
     Bund 24–5
     as minority religion 22–5
     Pale of Settlement 22, 24
     pogroms 24–5
July Days 60
justices of the peace 15

K
Kadets 12, 19, 35, 52, 65
Kamenev, L. 60, 104
Kerensky, A. 57, 59–60, 63, 79–80
Kirov, S. 110–11
Kochan, L. 66
Kolchak, Admiral 82–3
Komsomol 107
Korea 28–9
Kornilov affair 60–1
Kornilov, L. 61
Kotkin, S. 101
Kotlin Island 87
Kronstadt rising 87
kulaks 87, 111, 114–17
Kuropatkin, A.N. 28, 50

L
labour camps 87
   see also Gulag camps
Labourist Party 35
Lamsdorff, V.N. 28
land
   captains 15–16
   compulsory redistribution 35, 37
   distribution 59, 78
Lane, A. 90
Latvia 47, 62
legal system, influences on 25
leisure, and communism 108
Lena Goldfields massacre 12, 36, 39, 52
Lenin, V.I. 12, 20–1, 59–60, 63–5, 74–8, 86, 90
   assassination attempt 82
   death of 91
   ideology 92–3
   as leader 93–4
   opposition to 79–80
   Political Testament 103, 105
   poor health 103
   strengths 94
   weaknesses 94
Lenin Enrolment 93, 105
liberals 12, 16, 18–19, 65
living conditions 39, 40, 54, 66, 80, 115
Lvov, G. 59

M
Machuria 28–9
Martov, J. 20
Marx, K. 19–20
Marxism 19–20, 23, 46, 104
Marxism-Leninism 87, 92
Marxism-Leninism-Stalinism 101
Masurian Lakes 47
McCauley, M. 58
mechanisation 115
Mensheviks 12, 20–1, 24, 54, 65, 75
Michael, Grand Duke 54
Military Revolution Committee (MRC) 63–4
military
   incompetence 29
   militarisation of labour 86
   mutinies 32, 54
   Red Army 80, 82, 83–7, 110
   Soviet Order No.1 54
   see also First World War; police state
Milyukov, P. 19, 32, 56
Ministry of Finance 17
Ministry of Internal Affairs 17–18
minorities groups 22–5, 61, 80
mir 17, 37
Muslims 24
Mussolini 65
mutiny 32, 54

N
Narodniks 19
National Democratic Party 23
national minorities *see* minority groups
nationalisation 78, 86
nationalism 22–3
'Nepman' 90
New Economic Policy (NEP) 88–91
New Soviet Man 108–9
newspapers 107
Nicolas II
   abdication 48, 53–6, 66
   abilities 13–14
   anti-Semitism 24–5
   attitude 13
   as autocrat 13, 15
   character 12–13
   diaries 13
   downfall 50–3
   economic problems 16–17
   execution of 82–3
   family 14
   influences on 25–7
   opposition to 18–25, 30–2, 50–1
   overview of 12
   political problems 15–16
   religion 13
   social challenges 17–18
   Tsarina Alexandra 48, 51–2, 53
Nomenklatura 92

O
October Manifesto 12, 13, 19, 25, 27, 33–4
October Revolution 63
Octobrists 12, 19, 52
Odessa 32
Okhrana 31
Orgburo 88
Orthodox Church 25, 31, 51
Ottoman Empire 47

P
Pale of Settlement 22, 24
Pasternak, B. 108
peace, First World War 58, 77
peasants 13
   collectivisation 115–16
   land distribution 35, 37, 59
   land reforms 32
   poll tax 17
   population 17
   productivity 16
   union 32
   see also kulaks
Peasants' Land Bank 17
People's Commissariat for Internal Affairs (NKVD) 110
'People's Will' 15
Permanent Revolution 104
Petrograd 48
   see also St Petersburg
Petrograd Soviet 54, 57–8, 63
petty bourgeoisie 89
Pipes, R. 67, 122
Plehve, V. 19–20, 28, 30
Plekhanov, G. 20
plenipotentiaries 114
Pobedonostsev, K. 12, 25–6
pogroms 24–5
Poland 23, 83

Index

police
   centralised control of   15
   secret *see* Cheka
   state   109–12
Polikanov, N.   51–2
Polish Revolt (1863)   23
Politburo   88, 104, 111
political system
   Article 87   35
   autocratic system   15–16
   challenges to   17–18
   communism   54, 92–3
   constitutional changes   93
   decrees   77–8
   democratic centralism   92
   elections   74
   Fundamental Laws   12, 13
   in 1914   38
   October Manifesto   12, 13, 19, 25, 27, 33–4
   proportional representation   74
   Provisional Government   36, 53
   reform   12, 13, 34–5, 37, 58–9
   single-party dictatorship   76
   zemstva   15–16, 18
   see also Constituent Assembly; Dumas; Provisional Government
population   39
   national minorities   22–3
   rural   17
Populism   19, 24
Port Arthur, Siege of   28–9
Portsmouth, Treaty of (1905)   29
posters   107
post-Stalinist era   13
Potemkin   32, 108
poverty   15
Pravda   60, 63, 105, 107
Prince Georgy Lvov   59
Princip, G.   46
productivity   16
Progressists   52
'Progressive Bloc'   52, 55
proletariat   13, 17, 23, 65
propaganda   106–9
proportional representation   74
'Protocols of the Elders of Zion'   25
Protopopov, A.   51
Provisional Government   36, 53, 55–63, 73
   opposition to   61
   weakness of   64
Prussia   47
public health problems   17
purging   110–11
Putilov strike   31
Pyatakov, G.   111

Q

Queen Victoria   51

R

Radek, K.   111
railways   26–7, 29, 38
   impact of First World War   50
Rasputin, G.E.   48, 51–2
Red Army   80, 82, 83–7, 110
Red Guard   60–1, 64
Red Terror   86, 87
religion
   divisions in   24
   Holy Synod   25–6
   Russian Orthodox Church   25, 31, 51
Rennenkampf   47
repartition of land   17
retail trade   89–90
Reutern, M.   26
revolution, definition   34
Revolution (1905)
   Bloody Sunday   30–2
   causes of   30–4
   consequences   34
   strikes   31, 33
Revolution (1917)   53–65
   Bolshevik revolution in Petrograd   63
   causes of   62
   consequences of   65
   July Days   60
   October Revolution   63
revolutionary defencism   58
Riga   24, 47
   Treaty of   83–4
rioting   15
Rodzianko, M.   19, 54
Rogger, H.   40
Romania   32
Romanov dynasty   12, 13, 38, 46, 54
rouble   26
   see also currency
royal family, execution of   82–3
rural
   population   17
   unemployment   17
   unrest   16, 17
   see also agriculture; peasants
Russian Empire   22
Russian Orthodox Church   25, 31, 51
Russian Soviet Federative Socialist Republic (RSFSR)   86, 93
Russification   22–4
Russo-Japanese War   26, 27–30
Rykov, A.   103

S

sanitation   17
   see also living conditions
Sarajevo   39
Schlieffen Plan   46
'Scissors Crisis'   90
Second All-Russian Congress of Soviets *see* Congress of Soviets
secret police *see* Cheka
serfs, emancipation of   15
Sergei, Grand Duke   19–20, 31–2
Service, R.   100
sewerage   39
show trials   110–11
Siberia   27
Slavophiles   16, 26
slogans   63, 107
   see also propaganda
Smith, S.   96
Social Democratic Workers' Party (SD)   12, 19–21
Socialism in One Country   104
socialist organisations   17
Socialist Revolutionary Party   12
Socialist Revolutionary Party (SR)   12, 19, 65, 75, 82
Soviet Order No.1   54
soviets, establishment of   32–3
St Petersburg   40, 48
   see also Petrograd
St Petersburg Soviet   32–3, 64
Stakhanovite movement   108
Stalin, J.   13, 59, 65, 77, 91
   abilities   101–2
   agricultural policies   113–17
   character   100–1
   collectivism   104
   cult of personality   107
   industrial policies   118–21
   police state   109–12
   propaganda   106–9
   rise to power   102–6
State Capitalism   78, 86, 88
state *see* political system
Stavrou, T.G.   52
Steinbeck, J.   107
Stolypin, P.   12, 24, 35, 37, 40
'Stolypin's neckties'   37
Stone, N.   48
strikes   31, 33, 36, 52, 54
Struve, P.   18–19, 30
student unrest   30, 32
'substitution' effect   26
suffrage   73
Supreme Economic Council (SEC)   78

T

Tannenberg   47
Temporary Committee   56
terrorism   21, 28, 37
Thatcher, I.   60
timeline   11, 44–5, 72–3, 99–100
Togo, Admiral   29
trade   89–90
   see also economy
trade unions
   Assembly   31
   establishing   32
Transcauscasia
transport   26, 30, 80
   impact of First World War   50
   see also railways

Index

Trans-Siberian railway 27, 29, 38
Treaty of Brest-Litovsk 47, 77, 82
Treaty of Portsmouth (1905) 29
Treaty of Riga 83–4
Trebilcock, C. 27
trials, show 110–11
Triumvirate (*Troika*) 103–4
Trotsky, L. 32, 47, 60, 63–4, 82, 87, 90, 104–5
Tsarina Alexandra 48, 51–2, 53
tsarism
 opposition to 15–16, 18, 50–1
 and religion 13
 support for 67
Tukhachevsky, M. 110

U

Ukraine 23, 61, 80
underemployment 17
unemployment 17
Union in Defence of the Constituent Assembly 79
Union of Liberation 18–19
Union of Unions 32
unions *see* trade unions
United Opposition Group 104
United Soviet Socialist Republic (USSR) 93
United State Police Administration (OGPU) 109
universities, restrictions on 32
unrest 29–30, 33
 see also revolution
urbanisation 15, 17, 30, 39

V

Vilnius 47
Vyborg Manifesto 35
Vyshnegradsky, I. 16

W

'wager on the strong' 37–8
wages 40
Waldron, P. 36
war bonds 49
War Communism 80, 86, 92
Ward, C. 103
water supplies 17
Westernisers 16, 18, 26
Westwood, J.N. 35, 56, 90, 111
What Is to Be Done? 20
White armies 82–6
Witte, S. 12, 25, 26–7, 33, 51
women
 in Gulag camps 112
 votes for 73
worker demands 59
working-class consciousness 39
world revolution 88
writers 108–9

Y

Yagoda, G. 110
Yalu River, Battle of 29
Yezhov, N. 110
Yudenich, N. 83

Z

zemstva 15–16, 18, 32
Zinoviev, G. 103, 104
Zubatov, S.V. 21